THE LIBRARY
ST. MARY'S COLLEGE OF MARYLAND
ST. MARY'S CITY, MARYLAND 20686

087647

GIOVANNI BOCCACCIO'S

Nymphs of Fiesole

Other Works by Joseph Tusiani

THE COMPLETE POEMS OF MICHELANGELO
LUST AND LIBERTY: THE POEMS OF MACH-
　IAVELLI
RIND AND ALL (*poems*)
THE FIFTH SEASON (*poems*)
ENVOY FROM HEAVEN (*a novel*)
DANTE'S *INFERNO* (*for young people*)
DANTE'S *PURGATORIO* (*for young people*)
TASSO'S *JERUSALEM DELIVERED* (*a modern
　verse translation*)

GIOVANNI BOCCACCIO'S
Nymphs of Fiesole

TRANSLATED INTO VERSE AND WITH AN INTRODUCTION BY

Joseph Tusiani

RUTHERFORD • MADISON • TEANECK
Fairleigh Dickinson University Press

© 1971 by Associated University Presses, Inc.
Library of Congress Catalogue Card Number: 71-139989

Associated University Presses, Inc.
Cranbury, New Jersey 08512

ISBN: 0-8386-7835-1
Printed in the United States of America

for
Joanna Mondini

INTRODUCTION

This first verse translation of *Il Ninfale Fiesolano,* Giovanni Boccaccio's greatest poem and, undoubtedly, the best of his minor works, does not presume to find and present to the English-speaking world any startling new feature in the personality of the author of the *Decameron.* Its only aim is to shed light on a poem that, for its charm as well as its ease, should, indeed, occupy a prominent place in the literary history of fourteenth-century Italy. Caught, so to speak, between the majestic allegory of Dante's *Divine Comedy* and the mellifluous humanism of Petrarch's *Canzoniere,* Boccaccio's *Ninfale Fiesolano* creates none the less its own magic, and, unexpectedly yet inevitably paves the way for that popular vein which was to triumph in the narrative poetry of Luigi Pulci, Matteo Maria Boiardo, and Ludovico Ariosto.

Giovanni Boccaccio wrote more verse than prose in a century made great by the two poets he adored—Dante and Petrarch. It was perhaps his deep reverence for such masters that convinced him that no comparison was ever possible between their flight and his humble steps on Mount Parnassus.

> And when the savage steepness of the slope,
> and my most grievous life, and my gray hair
> convinced me that I never could get there,
> defeated, I abandoned every hope,
> and let all thoughts, all rhymes and verses go:
> so what I knew I now no longer know.[1]

But he did not abandon poetry altogether or, perhaps, poetry did not abandon him. It was, rather, a question of finding and being himself, and writing in the one way he knew—in the simple, colloquial, tongue-in-cheek, and self-amusing tone that fully revealed his personality. Poetry, as he came to understand it, was not the painstaking, fastidious, glittering conglomeration of mythological lore such as he had amassed in his *Teseida;* nor was it merely the scrupulously polished artifact of some of his *Rime.* Poetry had to be much less and yet much more than all that, if it wanted to be alive. So, for a change, he wrote as he felt. And so his *Ninfale Fiesolano* was born.

Written most likely in 1346, and definitely before 1348,[2] this poem is so different from the rest of Boccaccio's works that it is much easier to compare it with the best pages of the *Decameron* than it is to examine it in the light of his previous verse production. Simple in plot, the *Ninfale* has its point of departure in the enmity of Venus and Diana, yet owes nothing to Greek mythology, for, from its enchanted beginning, it creates its

---

1. *Rime,* CVII. "Mentre sperai e l'uno e l'altro collo." All the translations are my own.
2. A manuscript copy of the *Ninfale,* of 1473, bears in its *explicit* the year MCCCLXVI as its date of composition. However, an earlier reference to the poem found in a *canzone* by Matteo Frescobaldi, who died in 1348, allows one to think of the copyist's erroneous transposition of an "X" in the Roman number cited above. Cf. Vincenzo Crescini, *Contributo agli studi sul Boccaccio.* Turin, 1887.

own aura—a Florentine myth made of Florentine nymphs and Florentine shepherds. It employs in its development the devices of the ancient fables, yet it proceeds in absolute freedom from all that can be found either in Ovid or in Statius.[3] It seems to have nothing new to say, yet everything it says sounds so new as to seem invented by the first poet for his first enraptured audience. The secret, then, is not so much in the story as in something above and beyond the story itself; not in its loose and lucid *ottava rima* but in what keeps it lucid and loose; and not in its total lack of labor but in the artistry that gives it such felicitous release from restrictions of all kinds. But let us first look at the essential lines of the poem, which Francesco de Sanctis called "a hymn to nature."[4]

Africo, a twenty-year-old shepherd living at the foot of the hills of Fiesole, falls in love with Mensola, a beautiful fifteen-year-old nymph sacred to Diana. From slope to slope, he searches for her in vain, till, taking pity on his suffering, Venus appears to him in a vision and promises to help him. From valley to valley he resumes his quest, but none of the nymphs he encounters can tell him where Mensola lives or how he may meet her again. One day, he sees her from afar, and his love grows suddenly deeper in spite of a spear menacingly hurled at him by the beguiling maiden. Days and days elapse, and nothing can ever assuage Africo's grief. Goddess Venus appears to him again, and tells him what to do to win the heart of his cruel nymph. Following

---
3. Cf. Ovid's Epistula XI of the *Heroides* and Statius's *Achilleid* for possible similarities. See, also, for the other sources, Maggini's "Ancora a proposito del *Ninfale fiesolano*," in *Giornale storico della letteratura italiana*, LXI (1913): 32–40.
4. Cf. *Storia della letteratura italiana*. Milano: Universale Economica, 1950, 3:65.

her advice, he dons his mother's dress and, disguised as a nymph, goes once again in search of Mensola. He finds her in the midst of her companions chasing a wounded wild boar, which he slays. Praised for his courage by Mensola and the other nymphs, he joins them. Finally, they come to the bank of a stream where he, too, is invited to disrobe and bathe in the refreshing waters. Here comes the inevitable, for, at the sight of his masculinity, the nymphs scatter in terror. And here, too, Africo grabs his Mensola and fulfills his dream. Oh, the infinite tears of the sweet young nymph! She wants to die, having so displeased Diana. But Africo comforts her, and even succeeds in making her yield to him once more before they depart. They swear to see each other again the next day but fate decrees otherwise. The next day, and the next, and for one full month, Africo returns to the same place, waiting and waiting for his beloved Mensola. Then, driven by despair and unwilling to live another day without the object of his desire, he lets himself fall on his spear, and dies. Terrified by her sin, Mensola, in the meantime, does not know what is happening to her. Surely some mysterious illness is punishing her for the breach of her vow of chastity, for her body is swelling, her cheeks have lost their crimson hue, and there is no vigor left in her. Afraid of meeting her friends lest her sin should be known and reported to Diana, she finds solace in thinking of Africo. But one day she resolves to see Sinedecchia, an old nymph dwelling in a cavern nearby. She learns from her that she is expecting a child, and is told what to do. When her time comes, Mensola is delivered of a handsome infant boy, the perfect image of Africo. But at about this time, Diana returns to the hills of Fiesole to visit with her nymphs. All are summoned to convene but Mensola does not dare to face the Goddess. Diana herself, escorted by three nymphs, sets out for the cavern of the hapless girl. Not finding her there, she begins to go down the hill toward the river, calling out her name. In terror, Mensola hides her child among some bushes and starts fleeing in the direction of the stream, finally reaching it and jumping into its current. But the wrathful Goddess sees her and, made suddenly aware by the infant's piercing screams of the unpardonable sin committed in her absence, turns the unhappy nymph into the very water she is crossing. So ends Mensola, but not her child, destined for a triumph almost as great as his parents' woe.

But a poet's task is to raise his story to a level of lyricism. The story as such, that is, must be the mold into which to pour the molten gold of imagination and fantasy, of passion and pathos, and of character and charisma. This Boccaccio achieves by adding all of himself to his tale or, rather, by transmuting it into what he knows, and how he feels, about life and death, love and loss. The real metamorphosis is, perhaps, not that of Mensola but that of the poet who, while remaining a narrator, becomes, so to speak, the very world he narrates.

The *Ninfale Fiesolano* is, clearly, a convincing demonstration of Boccaccio's love for his Florence. He places his city in the ideal atmosphere of a primitive golden age in which man's passion, not yet channeled and tamed by society, blends with the beauty and strength of rivers and trees with a name and a life of its own almost above the existence of man himself. Thus he creates a Florentine pre-history of sheer grace and innocence, an Italian Arcadia where every stream has an enchanted legend of love, and a state, more than a place, of ineffable contentment and rest—an Ultima Thule of earthly delight. Boccaccio's lifelong fascination with rivers and lakes, mountains and forests,[5] finds in this poem its own habitat, and grows into such an infectious belief that it makes the reader pause in awe at the very mention of the tiniest brook or the sturdiest oak tree. Consequently, the nymphs of this hyperborean world are somewhat dissimilar from those of classical Greece. They wear the same apparel, are ruled by the same goddess, hunt and live in the same fashion, yet are not Greek; they are typical Florentine girls in love with nature, warm in spite of themselves, and so ravishing and intriguing as to make Boccaccio see nymphs wherever he chances to be.[6]

But the poem is more than all this. It is, above all, a real world in which Girafone and Alimena, Africo's aged parents, are so tender, so practical and down-to-earth, that they look like two characters created not by Boccaccio but by life itself. There is nothing dreamlike about them for their role is not only to counteract but also to stress their son's enchantment by the very nature of their daily existence. But from their innocent unawareness of Africo's suffering springs a poem-within-a-poem that, while relieving the tension, makes its causes more deeply felt and its consequences more easily foreseeable.

Alimena's concern for her son is unforgettable:

But in the meantime his resourceful mother
had gathered a large quantity of herbs
to make a bath with which she hoped to cure
the pain she thought her son felt in his side.
For how was she to know that something else

---

5. Cf. *De montibus, silvis, lacubus, stagnis seu paludibus et de nominibus maris liber,* one of Boccaccio's Latin works.
6. Cf. the *Ninfale d'Ameto* and, also, the *Caccia di Diana.* In the latter, Boccaccio refers to several Neapolitan ladies as "Diana's escorts."

was causing all that anguish and lament?
While she was readying her medicine,
her husband, Girafone, entered in.

He asked at once about his dearest son,
if he had come, that day, back from the wood.
His woman (Alimena was her name)
told him that he was home, and added soon
that he had found her words so wearisome
that she had better leave the lad alone,
and let him sleep. "Therefore, I think it's best,"
she said, "not to go up, and let him rest.

"I have prepared what's best for such a pain—
a most effective bath, I do believe.
When he has rested as his heart desires,
I'll bathe all of his body with this thing.
This is a bath that eases every pain,
and will completely heal him everywhere.
But let him rest as long as he desire,
for, when he talks, his pain grows so much higher."

Unforgettable, too, is Girafone's warning to his son. He knows life, and can therefore assure his Africo that love for a nymph can lead but to disaster. It is at this point that, to conceal his passion from his father, Africo tells a story that is both a true confession and a marvelous piece of fiction. In five *ottave*, Boccaccio gives us something comparable in spirit and overtones to such famous ballads as "Bonny Barbara Allan" and "Lord Randal" of the later Middle Ages.

"Father, O Father, a long time ago
I saw a youthful hind among these hills.
So beautiful was she, so fine and fair,

I'm sure the like was never seen before.
Certainly, God himself with his own hands
made that young doe so graceful and so sweet.
As nimble as a crane I saw her go,
oh, much, much whiter than the whitest snow.

"In love with her, I wished to catch her: so
from wood to wood I chased her a long way.
But to the mountain suddenly she flew,
and I, unable to pursue her still,
remained below with anguish in my soul.
Yet in my heart I knew I'd find her soon,
and that I had to start my chase again:
so I came home, and left the forest then.

"To tell the truth, as soon as I awoke
this morning, and I saw the sunshine break,
my mind was filled with thoughts of my sweet hind,
and I decided to resume my search.
So, all alone upon a lonely road
I went, and found myself, I know not how,
halfway above the hill when, warm and bright,
the noonday sun poured down its fullest light.

"Suddenly, I could hear as well as see
the leaves of some fresh oaklings faintly stir.
Holding my breath, and hidden by some rocks,
nearer and nearer drew I then, to spy:
three gentle hinds were feeding on the grass.
Thinking that I would now catch one at least,
to lure them, in my hand some tufts of grass,
silently, slowly toward them I did pass.

"But as they spied me, they began to run
fast up the hill, and waited not for me.

Seeing myself so mocked and left behind,
both grief and anger in my heart I felt.
But for a long, long time I chased them still,
bearing no other weapon than my own.
I stopped my chase when the descending night
removed them altogether from my sight. . . ."

Girafone and Alimena remain real people in a real, everyday world, too deeply familiar with a history of ancestral grief to forget themselves or be forgotten in the fleeting ease of a ballad, and, at the same time, too simple and unsophisticated to restrain their tears at the hour of tragedy. Yet there is majesty in their simplicity, and an extraordinary solemnity in their ordinary behavior in the face of death. When Girafone removes the fatal spear from the breast of his only son, and when he carries his lifeless body home, he is, more than a father, mankind itself surrendering to fate. And when Alimena, bemoaning her loss, falls on Africo's body and presses her face against her son's, she is, more than a mother, earth itself in its anguished unwillingness to relinquish the power of life. The reality of such human sorrow makes itself more keenly felt than even the untimely deaths of both Africo and Mensola, the youthful protagonists of the story.

The *Ninfale Fiesolano* is a celebration of youth and its natural instincts and impulses. More than Mensola, Africo discovers his own desire, and mistakes his whole life for it. On the other hand, more than a man named Africo, Mensola discovers her own power to conceive. It is nature discovering itself in the behavior of its creatures. Sex, therefore, is synonymous with innocence in a world where fountains sing in the shade and flocks feed free on the grass. The same force that causes the hills of Fiesole to rebloom in springtime makes Africo look for his Mensola. There is, or should be, no other explanation. But the first ominous shadow has already descended upon this world: its names are honor and loyalty. There is already in the air the sound of a new, incomprehensible word—sin. There is Diana already fighting against Venus. Fountains and flocks are blissfully unaware of the meaning of chastity; and so is Africo. But, unlike flocks and fountains, Africo is forced to duel with a phantom he cannot understand, for neither Plato nor Christ exists in his world. His only knowledge of both the world and himself is that he must be with Mensola. He has been told by his father that loving a nymph can lead but to disaster; but Mensola is a woman to him, not a nymph. If Diana means religion, and religion the loss of happiness he has experienced in Mensola's arms, then he is not afraid of Diana—or death. He is youth itself rebelling against anything that opposes its natural growth. And, indeed, the whole world about him reminds Africo of his youth. Mensola never appears alone but always escorted by youthful companions. She is only one of the beautiful nymphs of Fiesole, though she means more than all of them to Africo.[7] She sports, and eats, and laughs with others until the day of her sin; and her death is lamented by many a nymph from hill to hill. There is only one person, in Mensola's world, who has outgrown and outlived the

---

7. The title of Daniel J. Donno's prose translation, *The Nymph of Fiesole* (Columbia University Press, 1960) fails, in my opinion, to translate this idea of plurality implied in Boccaccio's. The Italian word "Ninfale," as "decennale," "corale," etc., connotes collectivity. Furthermore, it seems that even in his second "Ninfale," *Ninfale d'Ameto,* Boccaccio wanted to describe a pastoral world in its entirety rather than, or together with, the allegory of a single shepherd.

carefree naïveté of youth—Nymph Sinedecchia, famous for both her age and wisdom.[8] But, like Africo's parents, Sinedecchia emphasizes, by sheer contrast, the very world to which she seems no longer to belong. Her role in the story is by no means secondary, for it is she who intervenes when the two protagonists have perished, and thus assures the continuation of youth over and above Diana's rules of death. It is hard to imagine Pruneo's ultimate triumph without Sinedecchia's visit to Africo's bereaved parents in their lonely valley.

As has been said above, Boccaccio's personality is fully revealed in this poem. But this does not mean that he had a particular nun in mind in his delineation of fifteen-year-old Mensola.[9] The *Ninfale Fiesolano* is too broadly elemental to become strictly autobiographical. Boccaccio's personality is to be found, instead, in the sum total of the details that give scintillation to his style—his ability to prolong a description without diluting it, his power of analysis, his tendency to exaggeration, his Olympian smile through every line, and, more than once, his famous humor exploding noiselessly yet with lasting reverberation. The Boccaccio of the *Decameron* is already, *in toto*, in this poem, so much so that it would not sound atrociously farfetched to affirm that he had his major work in mind at the time of composition of the *Ninfale Fiesolano,* and that perhaps he even started in verse what he was to continue in prose. Certainly at least one phrase from the *Ninfale* is quoted almost verbatim in

---

8. Following the edition of Enrico Bianchi (Giovanni Boccaccio, *Opere Minori.* Salani Editore, 1964), I have kept the transcription of "Sinedecchia," instead of "Sinidecchia," for it seems to me that Boccaccio may have had the Latin "sine diecula" in mind in describing the oldest of all his nymphs. For the rest, I have followed Vincenzo Pernicone's critical text of 1937.
9. For this theory, see Enrico Carrara in "Un peccato del Boccaccio," *Giornale storico della letteratura italiana,* XXXVI (1900): 123–30.

the *Decameron*.[10] The only possible thing in the *Ninfale* that does not inevitably flow into Boccaccio's masterpiece is the crudity of some expressions, the unwarranted roughness of some verses, and the unnecessary breach of syntax here and there in the text. To what extent Boccaccio revised and polished his poetry we do not know. Nor is it safe to maintain that in the case of the *Ninfale Fiesolano* he purposely refrained from the *labor limae* in order to keep on a colloquial level a work most likely intended as a *cantafavola* for the piazza. For even so, this would not excuse lines that the least inversion could easily have salvaged or full quatrains that a second reading could undoubtedly have made acceptable. One example suffices, from stanza 166:

> Acciò che tanta noia non ti desse
> E che tu torni com' esser suoi sano:
> E non può esser che qualche consiglio
> I' non ti doni buon, caro mio figlio.

But even such flaws as these are worth considering in the development of Italian poetry. Boccaccio's *Ninfale Fiesolano,* perhaps the best Italian novella, is nearly halfway between Dante's *Comedy* and Pulci's *Morgante* or Boiardo's *Orlando Innamorato*. Were it not for the outdazzling fame of the *Decameron,* this poem would certainly enjoy a far greater reputation not only in Italy but also in the entire literary world.

Brief mention should at this point be made of an almost forgotten Elizabethan version of the *Ninfale*

---

10. I am referring to the image of "Master Stock" in the scene of the rape, which Boccaccio incorporates in the Prologue to the Sixth Day of the *Decameron*. Incidentally, the word "Monteficalli," untranslatable in English, has been rendered as "Black Hill," for Boccaccio himself uses "Monte Nero" in the above-mentioned Prologue.

Fiesolano, based not on the Italian text but on a French adaptation of it.

Nothing is known of the Io. Goubourne who, in 1597, published a book entitled *A Famous Tragical Discourse of Two Louers....*[11] We know, however, that his prosaic rendering of Boccaccio's story adhered rather faithfully to Antoine Guercin du Crest's *Le Nymphal Flossolan,* printed at Lyons in 1556, which in turn adhered so little to the original that it was almost an altogether different tale. The essentials of the story are so hopelessly entangled with explanations, moralistic precepts, didactic interpolations, erudite digressions, and geographical and astronomical observations, that they become scarcely recognizable. Had Mr. Goubourne consulted the Italian text, he would probably have thought that not a poem had been translated but the lengthy sermon of some obscure preacher from Florence. One instance will be sufficient to show what becomes of one of Boccaccio's stanzas.

> A false religion in those times was spread
> of false and wicked, ever-vicious gods.
> So had that seed of falsehood multiplied,
> those people thought all of their gods to be
> as kind in heaven as they seemed on earth.
> To all of them and, most of all, to Jove,
> here also, as in every other place,
> they sacrificed with lavish feast and grace.

---

11. *A Famous Tragical Discourse of Two louers, Affrican, and Mensola, their liues Infortunate loues, and lamentable deaths, together with the of-spring of the Florentines. A History no lesse pleasant then* (sic) *full of recreation and delight. Newly translated out of Tuscan into French by Anthony Guerin* (sic), *domino Creste. And out of French into English by Io. Goubourne. At London. Printed by Ia. R. for William Blackman dwelling neere great North doore of Paules. 1597.*

And here is the result of the Du Crest-Goubourne Franco-British alliance:

> Neere unto Florence the Chiefe Cittie of the Tuscan Region, there is a village called Flossolan, situate at the foote of a little mountaine, bordering on the South side: a large Plaine, fertile and well seated though in former time but little. At the confines thereof, bee (*sic*) many houses neere adioyning together, in forme of a Towne, without Walls, Ditches, or other Fortifications, (at least) none such as now be used . . . The Italians also amongst others, were not altogether free from this follie, but religiouslie held and beleeued (as a thing more than sure) that those whom they worshipped for Gods, as Jupiter, Mercurie, Mars, Neptune, Vulcan, Bacchus, Venus, and such like, discended on the earth below at their pleasure, to conuerse with men, in sundry places.

What is interesting, however, is that Goubourne's book followed the 1566 English translation of the *Thirteen Questions* from the *Filocolo,* and preceded the first translation of the *Decameron,* which appeared in 1620 — a singular milestone, therefore, in the history of Boccaccio's fame outside of Italy.

In my translation, as the reader will have noticed from the few strophes quoted in this Introduction, I have rhymed only the concluding couplet of each original *ottava*. Obviously, the famous rhyme pattern ABABABCC is infinitely more musical than a mere ABCDEFGG. But, as all translators of poetry know, the practical device of six blank verse lines may enable one to remain as close as possible to the spirit as well as to the letter of the original text. Following such a device, which I found extremely convenient and, as I went on with my task, even rewarding, I knew that my major concern was with the music, the suppleness, the alliteration, and even the colloquial nuances of Boccaccio's hendecasyllabic line. I did not find myself compelled to resort to inversions, or to alter, if not to sacrifice altogether, a thought or an image for the tyrannical exigencies of the rhyme. Why, then, instead of adopting blank verse for the entire translation, did I decide in favor of the rhymed couplet? It seemed to me, after completing the first twenty-odd stanzas in blank verse, that something was missing. I could still hear, clearly and with a joyous feeling, the echoes of their original music; yet something was lacking. Was it color? Was it magic? Was it a sense of continuity? Was it the very aura of a narrative poem? It was then that, already aware of the lesser degree of peril in the rhyming of only two of the eight lines of each strophe, I started all over. Suddenly, as I reread the same twenty-odd stanzas, I felt that I had, almost miraculously, kept the arrangement of their original ABABABCC, so completely had each rhymed couplet succeeded in making me forget the nonrhyming of its preceding portion. In other words, I felt once again the incantation of narrative poetry, an incantation which Boccaccio's verse, and not at all my effort, will, I hope, be able to prolong in the reader's heart. For, as Boccaccio himself warns us at the conclusion of his work, the *Ninfale Fiesolano* is a love poem to be read only by people in love. In consecrating his tale to Cupid himself, he says,

> Let this my book be read by gentle souls,
> by those who bear your emblem on their brows,
> by sweet and humble and angelic hearts
> where you still reign in all your majesty.
> These, these alone will not despise your deeds,
> but will, instead, accept them with their praise.
> So take my book. I offer now to you
> what to your lordship is forever due.

College of Mount Saint Vincent

Joseph Tusiani

GIOVANNI BOCCACCIO'S
Nymphs of Fiesole

Nymphs of Fiesole

1. Love that has long been living in my heart,
   where he will dwell forever, bids me speak.
   With that high splendor he still holds it bound,
   and with those rays that proved my armor vain
   the day they pierced my spirit with the grace
   of those fair eyes because of which I must
   in darkness and in daylight weep and sigh,
   and in grave anguish consequently lie.

2. Love is the one that guides and rules my hand
   in the sweet tale I am about to write.
   Love is the one that makes me this endure,
   spurring my strength, and quickening my mind.
   Love, my one escort and my only light,
   grants me to say the glory of his fame.
   And it is Love that bids me tell and prove
   a very ancient story of true love.

3. Therefore, let him alone all honor claim,
   who with his inspiration aids my style.
   It was my lady sent him to me here,
   whose virtue makes all other virtues dim.
   Such is her worth, and such her wondrousness,
   her gentleness outwins all lesser grace:
   she would, indeed, every perfection be
   if she resolved to prove more kind to me.

4. Now every faithful lover I entreat,
   so that he be my most effective shield
   against all those who blame or envy me,
   and those who never knew love's company.
   And now, my dear, sweet women, all of you
   whose hearts are not as hard as frozen snow,
   oh, beg my lady, still so harsh and rude,
   to show less fierceness on my servitude.

5. Long before Fiesole was built and raised
   with wall and moat and heavy citadel,
   only a few inhabitants lived there,
   who deemed it best to gather on the height
   of the surrounding hills. The plainland lay
   abandoned for the difficulty caused
   by the abundant waters which, below
   the mountain, made a copious river flow.

6. A false religion in those times was spread
   of false and wicked, ever-vicious gods.
   So had that seed of falsehood multiplied,
   those people thought all of their gods to be
   as kind in heaven as they seemed on earth.
   To all of them and, most of all, to Jove,
   here also, as in every other place,
   they sacrificed with lavish feast and grace.

7. In those days, too, a goddess reigned supreme,
   who was Diana by all people called.
   Full many a woman held her service dear,
   especially those who, wishing to preserve
   their maidenhood, abhorred all sinful lust
   and to her cult devoted all their years.
   With festival and bliss she welcomed all,
   in woods and forests holding them in thrall.

8. Fathers and mothers, to fulfill their vows,
   offered their virgin daughters to the Goddess;
   and others did it for some gift or grace
   they had been granted through her precious aid.
   With open arms Diana welcomed all,
   so long as they were willing to maintain
   their chastity unsoiled, all men to shun
   and heed far from the world her wish alone.

9. Thus was this virgin goddess then adored
   throughout the world; but let us now go back
   to our green hills of Fiesole where, more
   than elsewhere, she was honored and revered.
   I wish to tell you of the lovely throng
   of all her virgins dwelling on those hills:
   nymphs all of them were called so long ago,
   and all went armed with arrows and with bow.

10. Diana had assembled on those hills
    a mighty number of such virgins fair
    though she herself came very seldom down
    to live among them in her human guise.
    She had too many maidens in the world
    to guard from evil and from harm of man.
    Yet when she came to Fiesole awhile,
    to all her virgins she unveiled her smile.

11. She was of such erect, majestic height
    as goddesses should be; her glance, her face
    shone brighter than the brightest star above,
    for truly seemed she made in paradise.
    Her radiance cast such live and lustrous flame
    no glance could ever rest upon its glow,
    and not with gold her silken hair was lit
    but with a hue created just for it.

12. She wore it more than often lightly loose
    over her slender neck; her dress was cut
    and tailored like a neatly flowing gown,
    so delicately woven and so fine
    it barely veiled her flesh but did not mar,
    however, all the whiteness of its glow.
    She often used a belt around her cloak
    which like the finest purple seemed to look.

13. Twenty-five years of age her youth revealed,
    twenty-five years exactly, not one less.
    She grasped her fatal bow in her left hand,
    and her fierce quiver on her right side hung,
    laden with darts whereby she struck the beasts
    and often slew all those audacious men
    who durst annoy her or molest and seize
    any of her sweet virgin devotees.

14. In such a guise Diana spent her time
    at Fiesole among her darling nymphs.
    Gracious and kind, and with most lovely ways,
    she would quite often all of them convene
    around fresh fountains or within the shade
    of verdant boughs when summer days were warm.
    In winter time she gathered them, instead,
    where still some sunshine on the lawn was shed.

15. Here she would then admonish each and all
    to persevere in their virginity;
    but other times she would recall the hunts
    on which they more than once had been together
    upon those hills, where many a savage beast
    they had pursued and ultimately slain.
    And her command was always that they should
    keep chasing more wild beasts from every wood.

16. Such was, as I have said, their wonted talk,
    for much they loved to speak of hunting bouts.
    But when Diana was about to leave,
    unfailingly she summoned forth a nymph
    to represent her always in their midst,
    and made the others at that moment swear
    ever her wish, her wish alone to cherish,
    if by her bow they did not want to perish.

17. So was the chosen nymph obeyed by all
    that they believed Diana to be there.
    Each of the group was clad in a thin cloak
    skillfully woven of the selfsame flax,
    and all had made with their relentless bows
    a number of wild beasts bow out of life.
    Some of them hurled their darts with such a speed
    they made the nimblest leopard slow indeed.

18. And so the merry month of May had come
    when lovely meadows glisten with new buds,
    sweet nightingales in every place and plain
    pour out in song the newness of their loves,
    and young men feel in their audacious bliss
    the warmest valor of their flaming hearts.
    'Twas then to Fiesole Diana came
    to show her gathered nymphs her holy frame.

19. Around a beautiful and limpid stream,
    blessèd with blooms and wreathed with tender grass—
    a place one still can see right at the foot
    of Mount Ceceri where the midday sun
    lays all its brightness just in front of it—
    near Fonte Aquelli (this is now its name)
    Goddess Diana chose that day to be,
    eager her every nymph once more to see.

20. So all of them were seated happily
    around the beautiful and limpid stream
    when one of them, a slender, graceful nymph,
    rose to her feet and started then to blow
    a horn that made the others listen: after
    she finished, on the verdant grass again
    with her companions she sat down and each
    awaited eagerly Diana's speech.

21. As she was wont to do, this time again
    the Goddess prompted each and every one
    to let no soul approach them anywhere,
    and, "If perchance you ever meet a man,
    abhor him as you would a bitter foe,
    so that against you he may use no force
    or sly deceit," she said. "If you're not pure,
    beware! quick death or banishment is sure."

22. While such a council was still taking place,
    a tender youth, whose name was Africo,
    (of twenty years of age or maybe less)
    happened to be quite near. His cheeks were smooth,
    his hair shone blond and curly, and his face
    resembled now a lily, now a rose,
    and now a luscious fruit. Not far apart,
    he with his parents shared a lonely hut.

23. There in the woodland where Diana stood
    this young man chanced to be, brought to that spot
    by his delight of walking on and on,
    when suddenly he heard some fair nymphs talk.
    Nearer and nearer to their words he drew,
    listening closely from behind a cave.
    He was, because of this fair stratagem,
    seen by no nymph, but seeing each of them.

24. He saw Diana taller than the rest,
    rigid in all her words and all her thoughts,
    frightening with her arrows and her bow;
    and clearly he could view her gathered nymphs,
    feasting their gazes in her pleasant mien
    but overwhelmed with reverence and fear.
    Humble and silent, every maiden sat,
    listening to Diana's every threat.

25. He saw Diana ordering one to stand,
    and Alfinea, whose name was called, arose.
    She was the one who, so the goddess deemed,
    outdistanced all the other nymphs in years.
    Diana said, "Now listen all of you,
    seated up here. This nymph shall take my place
    when I am gone. Her wish you must obey
    as if I had not gone from you away."

26. As Africo stood listening to this,
    he saw a nymph appear before his eyes.
    He gazed upon her lovely face awhile,
    and felt Love gnawing at his heart at once.
    Already he began to sigh, already
    full-flaming torches burned all of his soul.
    So sweet a longing charged his every vein,
    he watched and watched and watched his nymph
       again.

27. And to himself he murmured, "Who on earth
would ever be more fortunate than I
if I could have that maiden for my bride?
Surely my heart already makes me know
that no one would experience more bliss.
If of Diana I were not afraid,
even by force I'd make my dream come true,
for all the other nymphs could nothing do."

28. Pining in such a way, our loving youth
remained still hidden in the cooling leaves
till, noticing that evening now was near,
and that the sun was fading fast away
beyond the yielding limits of the sky,
Diana and her nymphs, all glad and gay,
rose to their feet and, not before too long,
took to the hillock, singing a sweet song.

29. As every nymph was ready to depart,
and, also, she whom he now loved so well,
Africo heard her very name called out,
"Mènsola, let us go!" She joined the throng,
and when she was in their sweet company,
they all together started to disband.
Each to her cottage went before the night,
and so Diana was no more in sight.

30. Mènsola was but fifteen years of age:
her hair flowed down in waving curls of gold,
and of pure white her linen garments were.
Such was the gleaming beauty of her eyes
that but to see them meant no more to grieve.
What lovely manners! What angelic face!
But a sharp arrow in her hand she bore.
Let us go back to our poor lad once more.

31. Africo stayed behind, dismayed and dazed,
    moaning in such a way as none may guess
    the quick departure of his fair-faced nymph,
    and only musing on his short-lived bliss.
    "Alas, alas," he thought, "my restful peace
    has suddenly become unhappiness,
    for I know not what art must I employ
    or where to look to find again my joy.

32. "Nothing I know of her who's wounded me,
    save that her name is Mènsola. Alone
    she's left me here, alone and baffled most.
    She has not even noticed me. If only
    she knew how much I love her, and what load
    of anguish Love has placed upon my back!
    Alas, fair Mènsola, where did you go,
    leaving in such distress your Africo?"

33. Then he sat down upon that very spot
    where earlier his lovely nymph had lain,
    and, as a greater and more ardent fire
    grew in his breast and conquered all of it,
    he more than once found solace in the game
    of hiding all his face deep in the grass.
    He kissed it often, saying, "You are blest,
    who by so fair a nymph have now been pressed."

34. And, sighing, so he moaned, "Alas! Alas!
    What ruthless fate, what dismal destiny
    has lured me to this magic place today!
    I was so carefree once. Now look at me:
    I am most wretched for a girl I love,
    a girl that threw me on a road of woe,
    and wants no part of this my lonesome walk:
    Love, only Love walks with me, and my luck!

35. "Oh, if at least she knew how much I love her!
If only she had caught one glimpse of me!
Yet I believe that, had she seen me there,
she would have grown afraid, seeing herself
desired by me or any living man.
And, I am sure, as fast as she could flee
she would have run away, being one of those
forever sworn to shun all men as foes.

36. "So how am I to act now that the worst
thing I could do is to disclose myself?
And am I not already worse than dead
if I keep silent, and allow this fire
ever to grow? To live, then, I want death,
which would annul so much despair and ache.
And death, I know, will not delay to come
if nothing stops this flaming martyrdom."

37. With these and other countless words of woe
our loving lad bemoaned his bitter fate.
Finally, when he noticed that the sun
had set already, and the firmament
trembled with stars, to his dismay he thought
that it was time to leave. For a long while
he hesitated; then he said, "Oh, why
is not tomorrow's sun already high?"

38. He rose and, walking slowly, walking slowly,
his mind oppressed with thoughts of deep regret,
he made his way along the lawn toward home,
no more the carefree youth he was at dawn.
In such a pensive, melancholy mood
he reached his house, which near the plainland lay,
a quarter mile away, or even less,
from where the fountain sang its happiness.

39. When he arrived there, all alone, forlorn,
    saying no word to his father and mother,
    to his small bedroom he went up at once.
    Sighing, he threw himself upon his bed,
    and there he longed and longed for the new dawn
    with not one wink of sleep throughout the night.
    Tossing and turning, he could only sigh,
    and call his Mènsola with every cry.

40. I do not want you, gentlemen, to think
    there were such mansions then as we have now.
    This only you must know, that in those days
    those folks were happy with a single hut.
    They used no mortar for the homes they built
    but only stone and wood, and there were those
    who kept on building (it sufficed their needs)
    cabins with walls of simple clay and reeds.

41. As few as four were the inhabitants
    who in that humble, little village lived
    down in the plain below the lower hills
    which at the foot of the great mountains lie.
    I must return you now to the great grief
    Africo felt. Nearly a month elapsed,
    and yet his Mensola he could not see
    though many a nymph he met along the lea.

42. Love, long accustomed to renewing grief,
    wanted the poor young man to suffer more.
    As soon as He perceived that all his fire
    had somewhat eased its fury in his breast,
    wishing to bind him with far stronger chains,
    and hold him fastened with a fiercer knot,
    He found at last a way (his will was there)
    to double conflagration and despair.

43. Therefore, one night, as he lay sound asleep,
Africo saw a lady in his dream.
Her brow resplendent with the morning sun,
she held a little child within her arms.
All naked, in his hand he clasped a bow,
and when he from his quiver took a dart,
and was about to hurl it, "Wait, my son,"
the lady said, "don't hurry with your fun."

44. And, turning then to Africo, she said,
"What evil luck, what foolish thought has so
burdened your mind, it causes you to shun
what you want most? If not through cowardice,
through negligence you've lost your Mensola,
for you seem not to care about her love.
Here you are, deeply saddened and depressed,
when happiness should be your only quest.

45. "Arise, then! Go, and search from slope to slope
all of these hills, and you will find your nymph.
You will behold her with her friends at last
as they go tracking the wild beasts for sport.
Yes, being fast and wise, they're hard to seize,
but you no doubt will catch the one you love.
And of Diana have no thought or fear,
for she's a thousand miles away from here.

46. "I promise you the fullness of my help,
which is so mighty no one can resist
so long as I give order to my son
to wound one, at my bidding, with his bow.
Love is the only science I have learned,
and of my knowledge such good use I make,
not only men I catch and win with love
but even helpless gods—and even Jove."

47. And then she said, "My son, open your arms,
and make him feel the warmth of your true worth.
Reach in his breast and in his frozen heart
and thaw the ice that is still hiding there.
And now, my darling son, oh, do for me
what you do best." At that, Love seemed to bend
with such determined violence his bow
he made both tips close to each other go.

48. Africo was about to plead for mercy
when, fast, he felt the arrow pierce his breast,
and, passing through, wound fatally his heart.
At once he woke, and soon his hand went there
where he was sure he was to find the dart:
there was, instead, a lancinating pain.
Where was the lady with her son, who had
so fiercely wounded, once again, our lad?

49. He could not see her: she had fled away
together with the slumber and the dream.
Because of the new wound that made it smart,
his heart was beating fast; and he recalled
how beautiful his nymph was as she left
the fountain, and now cherished in his mind
her gentle manner and her graceful bearing,
and these remembrances his soul were tearing.

50. Therefore, he said, "The lady I beheld
undoubtedly is Venus with her son.
If I've correctly understood her words,
she promised to make Mensola now share
the very pain that I have felt alone.
Oh, if she ever strays a fleeting while
from her companion nymphs, I'll do the rest:
I'll grab her willy-nilly to my breast."

51. Thus, all his love rekindled by desire,
Africo felt determined now to roam
in search of Mensola from stream to stream
until he found her. Basking in these thoughts,
he saw the beautiful new dawn arise,
whose splendor he had longed for through the night.
All, all alone, he left his cottage, fast,
and to old Fonte Aquelli came at last.

52. Having arrived, he rested there awhile,
renewing all his bitter sighs of love.
"It was right here," he said, "Love's arrow struck,
and made me leave in anguish and dismay."
After he whispered so, he left the stream,
and started out along the lovely hill,
looking and listening if by any chance
he heard some breath or saw some nymph advance.

53. As he was climbing to the mountain top,
misled by love and swayed by his own thought,
he kept his forehead high, better to see
if anywhere the smallest object moved,
for, if he should at any moment chase
his sighted nymph, his legs were fast and strong.
Wherever a frail leaf was seen to stir,
rushed he, believing that a nymph was there.

54. But after nature more than once had fooled
with such apparent mockery our youth,
who still could see no living nymph appear,
suddenly, as he neared the mountain peak,
this thought flashed in his mind, "Why climb at all
if there is not one trace of her around?
It's nine o' clock already. No, ahead
I must not go, but take that road instead."

55. Guided by love and pensive still, toward Fiesole
he turned, and slowly down the slope he walked,
looking, forever looking for the one
whose harshness made him melancholy so.
But he had hardly walked a brief half mile
when to a most secluded place he came—
a valley that divided the two hills:
he heard nymphs singing, and he saw them, too.

56. Nearer to that deep valley soon he drew,
only to hear a sweet, angelic voice,
and then two more. He crossed his arms in prayer,
and, rapt in all that music, on his knees
he fell, and said imploringly to Jove,
"God, can perhaps my Mensola be found
among these nymphs on the brink of this brook?
I hope she's there, for I am going to look."

57. As one who wants to catch a cricket goes
with long, and nimble, intermittent steps,
holding his breath, so Africo now went,
moving from rock to rock along his way,
following after that sweet-echoing song
arising from the glen. Closer and closer
he came, until he could see oaklings stir,
behind whose leaves some nymphs and nymphets
were.

58. He drew still nearer, utterly unseen,
until he saw wherefrom the song was born.
Three nymphs he viewed, and each was singing still:
around the one who stood, the other two
sat near a rill that in a furrow flowed.
He caught a glimpse of their fair legs, for both
were washing then their white and wondrous feet
while countless birds around were singing sweet.

59. The other, who was standing, gathered leaves
wherewith she wove a garland for herself
which, then, she bound about her golden curls
so as to guard them from the harming sun.
And two more wreaths she wove, as thick and deep,
for her two friends; she placed them on their hair,
disheveled, and uncombed, and, one could see,
full of the foliage fallen from a tree.

60. Africo meanwhile murmured to himself,
"I am afraid my Mensola's not here."
He came still closer to the singing nymphs,
cursing his evil fortune in his heart,
and saying, "Venus, what you promised me,
if I see clearly, has not yet come true.
What shall I do now? I will face the three,
and ask them if they have some news for me."

61. Having therefore decided to disclose
himself to them, the young man walked straight on
to where they were, and then with quiet voice
and humble countenance he said to them,
"Oh, may Diana, sovereign of your hearts,
keep you forever adamant and chaste!
Beautiful nymphs, be not of me afraid,
but listen to me, for I need your aid.

62. "I have been searching for one of your throng,
whom Mensola you call, I do believe,
from hill to hill, from place to verdant place.
I have been looking for her one full month;
ah, but so harsh and fleet of foot is she
that always has she faded from my sight.
Therefore, I beg you, tell me where she is,
O dear and lovely sisters full of bliss."

63. Just as young sheep outside a shepherd's care
    run, if a wolf assails them, terror-struck,
    this way, that way—the dear, defenseless ones!—
    bleating *beh beh,* bewildered and dismayed;
    or just as silly hens are wont to do
    when suddenly a fox jumps in their midst—
    as fast as each can fly, all in a group,
    they run, run, restless, raucous, to the coop:

64. so the three beautiful and frightened nymphs
    ran as they saw a man. "Alas!" they screamed,
    and, to flee faster, lifted up their skirts,
    exposing thus their pretty, shapely legs.
    Poor Africo was granted no reply
    for, fetching fast their bows, as fast they went,
    two toward the hill, and one along the lawn:
    like hunted beasts they wildly ran and ran.

65. Africo shouted, "Wait, oh, wait for me,
    beautiful nymphs! Oh, listen to my word!
    I wish to tell you that I have not come
    to vex you or to make you die from fright,
    but only to invite you to rejoice
    so that you may not run away from me.
    Ah, as a loyal friend I've come to you,
    but you avoid me like a cruel foe."

66. But what's the use to plead, poor Africo?
    They are still running, running toward the hill,
    and in the valley you are left alone
    without the solace of one soothing word.
    So let them go; abandon your pursuit,
    since each of the three nymphs wants but to flee.
    Frightened and deaf to what you say, they go,
    and all your prayers find the winds that blow.

67. They had already sped so far from him
    he could no longer see them in their flight.
    Thus he decided to give up his chase,
    and started then bemoaning bitterly
    the strange behavior of those savage nymphs.
    "And now what shall I do?" he said. "I see
    no other means or way from them to gain
    anything but ingratitude and pain.

68. "To no avail keep I imploring them,
    yet silence, too, would serve me not at all.
    I cannot use my strength against a nymph,
    for willingly I'd do it if I could.
    Oh, if I only were allowed to see
    my Mensola, or know at least the place
    where I might look and find her finally!
    Instead, I blindly grope, and nothing see."

69. So greatly had his mind been seized and vexed
    by his long search of Mensola, and of
    the nymphs that in the valley he had found
    as they relaxed beneath a shaded bough;
    and so astray his chase had led his steps
    for some good news of Mensola at least
    that when night softly came he failed to mark
    the rim of the horizon growing dark.

70. Disconsolate, forlorn, he cursed himself,
    and cursed the sight of the approaching dark
    for coming, ah, so soon; then, slowly, down
    the hill, from den to den, he started out.
    He did not wish to tarry any more
    lest in the darkness he should have to fight
    any wild beast that wandered from its lair
    with poisoned fangs ever ready to tear.

71. So, having eaten nothing all day long,
    Africo started his slow journey home.
    Hour after hour, with anguish in his heart,
    his father had been waiting for him there.
    He was afraid that some wild beast had seized
    his darling son and killed him on his way,
    tearing him limb from limb for its gory meal;
    and now such lateness made his fear more real.

72. He also of Diana was afraid,
    a bitter foe of all his family.
    Therefore, he thought that she had met his son,
    and slain him or, to spite him even more,
    turned him into a rock or leafy tree.
    At this late hour, with grief deep in his heart,
    the worried father was awaiting him,
    and all his thoughts were desolate and grim.

73. The sun had fled into the western world,
    where, deep-concealed, its light was seen no more.
    The stars already with the shining moon
    were visible above the bluish air.
    Gone was the song of every nightingale,
    but those birds sang that ever shun the day
    and only sing when shadows darkly roam:
    at this late hour poor Africo reached home.

74. With indescribable delight and bliss
    the father welcomed his beloved son,
    for he had feared some predatory beast
    had hurt him with its claws along the way.
    And soon his pitying mother, still in tears,
    embraced him, saying, "Son, my lovely lily,
    where have you been all day, my son, my dear,
    to cause us so much anguish, so much fear?"

75. And then, in turn, his father wished to know
where he had been with nothing to eat all day.
Africo could not answer then and there,
thinking of any plausible excuse;
but Love, that sharpens a true lover's mind,
came promptly to his rescue, teaching him
something that seemed, indeed, a good reply.
Africo to his father told this lie:

76. "Father, O Father, a long time ago
I saw a youthful hind among these hills.
So beautiful was she, so fine and fair,
I'm sure the like was never seen before.
Certainly, God himself with his own hands
made that young doe so graceful and so sweet.
As nimble as a crane I saw her go,
oh, much, much whiter than the whitest snow.

77. "In love with her, I wished to catch her: so
from wood to wood I chased her a long way.
But to the mountain suddenly she flew,
and I, unable to pursue her still,
remained below with anguish in my soul.
Yet in my heart I knew I'd find her soon,
and that I had to start my chase again:
so I came home, and left the forest then.

78. "To tell the truth, as soon as I awoke
this morning, and I saw the sunshine break,
my mind was filled with thoughts of my sweet hind,
and I decided to resume my search.
So, all alone upon a lonely road
I went, and found myself, I know not how,
halfway above the hill when, warm and bright,
the noonday sun poured down its fullest light.

79. "Suddenly, I could hear as well and see
    the leaves of some fresh oaklings faintly stir.
    Holding my breath, and hidden by some rocks,
    nearer and nearer drew I then, to spy:
    three gentle hinds were feeding on the grass.
    Thinking that I would now catch one at least,
    to lure them, in my hand some tufts of grass,
    silently, slowly toward them I did pass.

80. "But as they spied me, they began to run
    fast up the hill, and waited not for me.
    Seeing myself so mocked and left behind,
    both grief and anger in my heart I felt.
    But for a long, long time I chased them still,
    bearing no other weapon than my own.
    I stopped my chase when the descending night
    removed them altogether from my sight.

81. "Now that you know what brought me home so late,
    Father, O Father, do not doubt my word."
    His father (Girafonè was his name)
    knew well what that mysterious fable meant,
    and, being wise and wary of the world,
    most clearly understood, and was convinced,
    that what his son had called fair, gentle does
    were real nymphs caught lying in repose.

82. But not to show he knew his son had lied,
    and to conceal that he had sensed the truth—
    for he would only make him much more eager
    to search for them again whereas, instead,
    he only wished that he might soon forget
    and tear his aching love out of his heart—
    he told him he believed what he had done.
    But it was he who then addressed his son:

83. "O my sweet son, my dear and only one,
ah, in the name of God, beware, beware
of such fair hinds as you have now described,
and let them all with all their curses go.
I know, and swear upon my very life,
that to Diana all of them belong,
and they at ease go feeding on these mountains,
drinking the cool, sweet waters of our fountains.

84. "Often Diana goes along with them,
bearing her arrows and her deadly bow.
Ah, if for your misfortune she should see you
pursuing one of them, she'd give you death
with one of her avenging darts, for often
have those who tried to harm her hinds been struck.
Besides, she is, and will forever be
the greatest foe of our old family.

85. "Alas, alas, it pains me still, my son,
to tell you how my hapless father died
now that all this reminds me once again
of how and where Diana took his life.
So may Jove help me, O my darling son:
the story of my father's sin is true.
Mugnonè was his name, as you know well,
but what you do not know I want to tell.

86. "This story, much too long, would never end,
were all details revealed of his sad fate.
But, to come quickly to its final act,
my father, too, would wander through these hills,
as hunters do, to track and wound wild beasts.
One morning, weary from his hunting chase,
he reached a valley and a lovely stream,
called ever since Mugnonè after him.

87. "When he got there, he saw a lovely nymph
rest near a lovely fountain all alone.
She saw him, and her brow grew pale from fear.
'Alas,' she moaned and, rising fast and frantic,
began to flee, so frightened yet so sweet,
with tenderness and terror down the hill.
My father begged her, begged her to remain,
but, when he saw his plea was all in vain,

88. "he started chasing her. O wretched man,
so unaware of your awaiting death!
You did not know, poor Father, you were soon
to fall into the snares of your own fate.
As you were running after your sweet nymph
with greater speed and strength, why did Diana
not think of turning her into a rock,
into a bird or bush or flowery stalk?

89. "No sooner had she reached the saving stream
than, weak and weary, out of breath and faint,
she dropped between her legs the silken slip
that she had gathered when her flight began.
Hapless, Mugnòn rejoiced: a few more steps,
and there the breathless nymph was caught at last.
He grabbed her, clasped her in his first embrace,
with kisses, kisses on her virgin face.

90. "There he used force and violence, and there
the helpless, overwhelmed, and frightened nymph
could not but yield to his deflowering lust.
Unhappy youth! O fair, ill-fated nymph!
You were united in each other's arms,
yet grief and anger kept you far apart.
Diana from the overhanging peak
saw the two sinners, fastened cheek to cheek.

91. "She shouted, 'I have caught you, wicked ones.
This is the time you shall go both to hell.
You will not see the winter of this year
for you will leave the world this very day.
Your names will ever linger in the stream
where you together may forever be!'
This said, the goddess with her faultless art
struck the two lying lovers with one dart.

92. "Diana's arrow and her final word
reached and transfixed the two at the same time.
I'm telling you no tales, my dearest son,
and I would be most grateful to the gods
if this heartrending story were a lie.
Thus the two lovers ended in one death:
one arrow pierced two hearts and made them still,
and so her shyness stopped, and so his will.

93. "And so it was my luckless father's blood
stained the whole river with a crimson hue:
flowing and carrying blood along its course
the water made the tragic story known.
His body lies still buried down its bed,
for no one ever saw it anywhere
or ever knew to what far shore it came:
only this river still retains his name.

94. "Diana—this is what I heard it said—
gathered her nymph's fair blood to its last drop,
brought it with her dead body near the stream
next to a lovely fountain, left it there:
she was determined to remind all men
who ever chanced to see that gory sight
how cruelly and fast her arrow runs,
striking all creatures who offend her once.

95. "Of thousands I could tell you, my dear son,
who are now birds and brooks among these hills.
Others, for having sinned against her, soon
were turned—unhappy ones—to shrubs and trees.
Do not forget that in our family
I lost two brothers, also by her hand.
Ah, in the name of God, beware, my son,
and from the vengeance of this Goddess run."

96. Old Girafonè ended thus his tale,
and still his bitter tears came streaming down.
Africo listened to his every word
with great attention, missing no detail.
Although the tale he had been listening to
had filled his heart with a foreboding fear,
his mind remained unchanged. "Father," he said,
"this won't occur again. Be not afraid.

97. "I promise to ignore them from now on
if young hinds chance to cross my path again.
And now, dear Father, let us go to rest,
for I am very tired, very tired
from traveling all day from hill to hill.
So many miles I walked, so many miles,
I thought I'd never see again this door.
Father, I beg you, talk to me no more."

98. They went to sleep, but when the new day dawned
Africo jumped out of his cot in haste,
and to his well-known hills returned once more
where both his heart and mind had lain all night.
Looking behind, ahead, and everywhere,
he wished to know where Mensola might be.
Finally, it was Love that bade him go
right where she stood as near as shot of bow.

99. But it was she who first caught sight of him,
whereat she hastened once again to flee.
Hearing her cry "Alas!" Africo looked,
and saw her fleeing fast from him away.
"I'm sure that's Mensola," he thought at once,
and started chasing her as fast he could.
Over and over, calling out her name,
he pleaded, "Wait! I love you. Please remain!

100. "Beautiful maiden, do not flee from one
who loves you more than he can love the world.
I'm one enduring for your love alone
a never-ending anguish, day and night.
I am not chasing you to give you death
nor, as you think, to harm you in the least.
Love, it is love that makes me follow you—
for enmity or hate I never knew.

101. "Not as the falcon that pursues the trembling
partridge in flight am I pursuing you,
nor as the greedy wolf eager to kill
the terror-stricken little lamb astray.
You, you alone are dearer to my heart
than anything I see and cherish most.
You are my hope and my desire, and, if
you suffer, I am part of your same grief.

102. "Oh, wait, my lovely Mensola, for me,
and by the gods I swear and promise you
that I will keep you as my sweet, young bride,
and love you, love you, love you as the one
who is my one delight, my only world,
and rules all of my feelings and my thoughts.
You are my solace and my only guide;
my life belongs to you, my lovely bride.

103. "Why then, O cruel heart, do you still want
to be the cause of my distress and death?
Why do you, with no reason, still remain
so deaf and so ungrateful to my love?
For loving you so much, you wish me dead—
is this the one reward you can bestow?
If I were not in love, what would you do?
You could not treat me worse, this much is true.

104. "Stop fleeing, then, or you're more pitiless
than a she-bear that feeds her little whelps.
You are, I tell you, bitterer than gall,
and much, much harder than a marble block.
But if you wait for me, you're sweeter far
than honey, sweeter far than sweet, new wine,
and more than any sun you're fair and bright,
so dear and charming, and so soft and white.

105. "But I can see my pleading is in vain,
for you heed not whichever word I say.
I am your slave and you seem not to care:
you do not even turn around to look.
Just like a dart that leaves the bow and flies
you shun my sight and through the forest flee,
utterly unconcerned in your retreat
with rock and bush that bruise your legs and feet.

106. "But since you're so determined, as I see,
to run away from one who loves you so,
and since all of my prayers seem to make
your cruel soul more pitiless and harsh,
may Jove—this only grace I ask of him—
turn into plainland all these hills and slopes,
a level, easy plain where you may meet
no rock or bush so harming to your feet.

107. "Oh, hear my plea, O holy gods who dwell
throughout these shady valleys and these hills!
Be kind, if kindness you have ever shown,
to the delightful, shapely, snowy legs
of my sweet nymph, and turn into soft grass
and lovely meadows stone and bush and tree
so that her delicate and dainty feet
may not be hurt by roughness that they meet.

108. "Look! I refrain from chasing you, my love.
Go where your heart desires, and go in peace.
In my unhappiness I'll be alone,
alone in all this endless restlessness,
until I reach the end of my despair,
for this my heart is soon to throb no more.
Little by little, all my years abate,
and it is you that rule my flaming fate."

109. So frightened and so fast the nymph ran on,
she seemed to fly. To flee with greater speed,
she thought of this device: her flimsy gown
she lifted up and bound around her belt,
whereby to those who might have chanced to look
she showed her legs full bare up to her knees:
a vision that would make all men who see
full of desire and mad with jealousy.

110. She carried still her arrow in her hand:
it was the dart that, after her long flight,
she chose to hurl. Emboldened by her fear,
she turned and, looking fixedly and stern,
threw that swift arrow with her valiant arm
to give a mortal wound to Africo.
Surely, it would have killed him, were it not
for an oak tree that took, instead, the shot.

111. Seeing her arrow whistling in the air,
 and gazing, in the meantime, on the face
 of her young lover, which, indeed, seemed made
 with every beauty born in paradise,
 suddenly she repented of her deed
 and, with great pity spying from afar,
 "Watch out, young man," she cried. "It is too late
 for me to save you from your cruel fate."

112. So straight and sharp the nimble arrow flew,
 and with so great a force it hastened down,
 it struck the sturdy oak and pierced it through
 as if it were an easy bank of snow.
 So massive was the tree, no man on earth
 could have encompassed it with his bare arms:
 it split wide open, laying bare its heart,
 by more than half the shaft torn, quick, apart.

113. Seeing her lover luckily unharmed,
 Mensola now rejoiced things went this way,
 for Love had snatched all harshness from her heart,
 and even made it heed his bidding might:
 not that she had by any means become
 eager to wait for him or vaguely thought
 of welcoming his love—but she was glad
 for being no more pursued by the young lad.

114. So once again she took to fleeing fast,
 oh, very fast away from Africo,
 who, begging, crying, and with quicker pace
 was running and still running after her.
 Passing from cave to cave, from slope to slope,
 she left him far behind and out of sight,
 until she reached the peak of the great hill:
 but safe not even there was she to feel.

115. Rapidly from that summit she went on
where the thick forest made the plainland dark.
Such was the thickness of the countless trees
that nothing was perceived within its midst.
Hiding in utter silence, there the nymph
remained awhile like a bewildered bird.
Deep in the greenness of fair oaklings weird
the timid maiden quickly disappeared.

116. But let's say more of Africo. As soon
as he beheld the nimbly flying dart,
he suddenly grew pale; but, hearing then
the young nymph warn, "Watch out! Watch out!"
  with sudden
compassion in the gleaming of her glance,
he felt a greater wound within his heart,
and, more than ever eager to pursue
his lovely maiden, to himself was true.

117. Just as a brand, already charred and spent,
with but a fainting spark left of its life,
suddenly lets a livelier fire shine,
and multiplies its might a hundredfold
if but a gust of blowing wind arrives:
such, as he heard her pitying word resound,
Africo felt at once. His hidden fire
was suddenly revived, and burned much higher.

118. Aloud he answered, "Since you want my death,
oh, would to Jove I were already dead!
Thus you would have fulfilled your one desire—
to see your arrow planted in my heart.
It went, instead, elsewhere through your mistake.
But your belated pity's of no use:
happier I would be if with your dart
you'd rescued me from what enflames my heart."

119. Africo had but uttered this lament
 when Mensola he finally saw reach
 the summit of the mountain: it was then
 she sought the other side and disappeared.
 She had a great advantage over him,
 and so he grieved, and sadness filled his heart.
 She was no longer within reach or view;
 therefore he feared he'd lost her—which was
    true.

120. Weary, and after much distress and pain,
 he climbed up there, and looked for her in vain.
 As hunters often do when the tracked beast
 fades altogether out of reach and sight—
 running that way and running back this way,
 they seem to have their foreheads everywhere,
 and other times they stop and only listen,
 thinking of nothing else and for one reason:

121. so on the great hill Africo behaved—
 lifting his glance and peering everywhere,
 wrathfully striking with his hand his brow,
 sighing, and cursing his horrendous luck
 for all the sorry trials of his life.
 Finally, deep into the wood he walked,
 only to come right out and in dismay
 say to himself, "Perhaps she went that way."

122. In that direction he would swiftly run,
 hoping to catch a glimpse of her at last;
 but, failing still to see her, sad and grieved,
 he would retrace his steps or move elsewhere.
 Wherever he now thought she might have gone
 he also went, in error every time,
 until he could not think at all or know
 what else to do or which new way to go.

123. And yet he kept repeating to himself,
"Perhaps she's hiding in this deep, dark wood;
and if she is, how can I find her now
unless I see a bush or something stir?
I would remain for a whole month and more,
searching these shady miles, tree after tree.
I cannot even imagine how she might
have entered here with not one path in sight.

124. "Nor can my heart advise me in the least
in which direction she may have escaped,
so many ways throughout this forest cross.
Yet if I stay much longer on one trail
I may but choose the wrong one, and perhaps,
in doing so forever lose my chance
of winning what I long so much to win.
Oh, what distress and anguish I am in!

125. Therefore, what shall I do—go home or wait
until I see her finally appear?
So thick and deep these woods and groves extend
that I believe a horseman could go through
without the slightest fear of being seen.
But even if she left her hiding place,
that might be almost a long mile away,
and I in vain would chase her all the way."

126. He looked then at the sun: it was about
three o' clock past noon. Africo thought and said,
"Since I have lost already every hope
of being with my love, as I had wished,
I want to leave this wilderness at once,"
for he remembered now what he had heard
only the day before from his own father—
how the two lovers had been slain together.

127. Love, on the other hand, so made him speak,
"Who cares about Diana and her threats?
If I fulfill my longing only once,
it is the fullness of my bliss that counts;
for if, to please my heart, I had to die,
I would thank God for such a happy death.
I only would be grieving for her fate,
were she to die for being my sweet mate."

128. With such and other thoughts now in his mind,
Africo lingered a while longer there,
not knowing what to do or what to say,
so much had Love ensnared and vanquished him.
Finally, he resolved he should not cause
his worried father any more dismay
by being out at night where wild beasts roam:
therefore, against his will, he went back home.

129. He started out so much against his will
that he looked back with every step he took.
Pausing awhile, he listened all intent
for any sound of Mensola around.
Ever he moaned, "Unhappy me! Alone
and empty-handed, unconsoled, I go—
and shall I leave you, Mensola, behind?"
But her, though he went back, he could not find.

130. It would be very, very long to tell
how many times he then retraced his steps,
forward and backward, once and once again,
for every stirring leaf he chanced to see;
and how, each time, his heavy heart was sore
with deeper sadness as he went away.
But, just to make a long long story brief,
he reached his home in great distress and grief.

131. Avoiding both his father and his mother,
he stole into his room immediately,
and threw himself upon his little bed,
with Cupid strong already in his heart.
So ruthlessly had Cupid wounded it
that he was more than willing now to die,
for death would free him from such hopeless strife
since he had lost the joy of all his life.

132. Stretched out upon his bed, Africo lay,
endlessly sighing and in endless ache,
so fiercely pricked by Love's relentless darts
that, "Oh, my God!" lamented he three times,
so loudly that his mother heard him moan.
In the small garden right beside their home
his mother at that moment clearly heard,
and hurried toward her son's lamenting word.

133. Upstairs she hastened to his little room,
for she had recognized the darling voice.
Greatly she was amazed to find her son
lying upon his bed in such a state.
Disconsolate, her voice broken with sobs,
she said, embracing him, "O son, dear son,
oh, tell me what it is that grieves you so,
and what is causing such a piercing woe.

134. "Oh, tell me quickly, O my blessèd son,
where, where it is you feel this sudden pain.
At once I will prepare a medicine
that, you will see, will heal you in no time.
Please, look at me, my darling, my sweet love,
and, for my sake, say something, O my dear.
I am your mother. For nine months, you know,
I carried you in me, and felt you grow."

135. Hearing his tender mother in his room,
Africo was annoyed and sorely sad
that she had caught him in his misery.
But, having been made shrewd and wise by Love,
he quickly thought of some good lie to tell.
Raising his head, he showed his tearful face,
saying, "This morning, Mother, on my way
back home, I fell, and hurt myself—this I can say.

136. "I soon got up, but such a pain I felt
here in my side I thought that I would never
make it this far. I was so weak and worn
that I could hardly stand upon my feet.
I fainted like snow melting in the sun;
but finally I made it to my bed,
and now the pain, believe me, is much less,
that gave me so much anguish and distress.

137. "So, if you love me, Mother, Mother dear,
leave me, I beg you, so that I may rest.
And, please, forgive me if I tell you this,
but I am pained by any word I say.
Besides, there's nothing you can do for me.
So, darling Mother, do not argue: go.
Do as I say, for any word, believe me,
is worse than poison and can only grieve me."

138. This said, he looked away and spoke no more,
but kept on sighing, sighing hopelessly.
Hearing all this, his mother stood awhile
baffled and apprehensive at his side.
She thought and said, "Indeed, it seems to me
that every word I utter grieves him more.
Perhaps it is my voice's very sound
that echoes where his pain is most profound."

139. She left the room, but still her only son
     lay with his ache and anguish on his bed.
     Seeing himself now finally alone,
     Africo started his complaints again
     about the torment that he felt and knew,
     and that by now was deeper in his breast
     than ever before. He moaned in endless woe,
     "From bad to worse, because of Love, I go.

140. "His inmost flames are burning all of me,
     and well I feel that their new might devours
     my breast, my heart, my life from everywhere.
     No one can help me, nothing can avail,
     nor can I ever for some solace hope.
     One person only can assuage my pain,
     only one person can, if she desire,
     give me some peace by quenching all this fire.

141. "You, you alone, my blond and comely nymph,
     so gentle and angelic, sweet and fair,
     fresh and bedewed far more than a white rose,
     clear and resplendent more than any star,
     upon this earth you are the only one
     whose charming winsome voice I so adore.
     You, you alone I call my sole delight
     at every moment of both day and night.

142. "You are the only one who can restore
     my happiness, and end my misery.
     The only one you are in whose sweet hands
     my life, no longer mine, will ever dwell.
     You are the one (and may your heart so wish)
     who can deliver me from cruel death.
     The only one you are, if so you care,
     who can right now annul all this despair."

143. And this he added, "O my wretched fate!
You are so cruel and so pitiless,
so unconcerned with suffering of men
that you dread those who merely look at you.
Instead of caring for this life of mine,
you keep it in a deep, dark dungeon thrust.
Alas, how can I ever make you know
what you can't see—my never-ending woe?"

144. Addressing holy Venus with a sigh,
he said, "O holy Goddess, who know well
how to resist and tame all human might
that dares oppose the triumph of your darts
so that no man may ever safely go,
it seems to me you cannot win this time
a tender girl who proves to be so great
as to defeat your love with all her hate.

145. "A girl, it seems, has so outvanquished you
you have lost all your power and your worth.
Cupid, your Son, with all the subtle art
with which he tamed both hard and gentle souls,
can nothing do against this stony heart
that mocks and makes so little of your might,
and spurns the bow and all the sharpened darts
whereby he made you triumph o'er all hearts.

146. "Perhaps you thought that you could win her, too,
as easily as you won this my life,
and that you could possess her icy breast
as you do mine with all your subtle wiles.
Instead, she blunted all the ruthless darts
with which in vain you tried to pierce her soul,
whereas, poor me!, being defenseless, I
in everlasting prison now must lie.

147. "Nor can I ever hope to be set free,
or to be granted peace or truce or rest.
I but expect my thoughts of love to grow
and, therefore, all this anguish to increase.
My tears and my despair ultimately
will cause my wretched soul to leave this flesh,
and face, against its will, its ghastly night:
and this will be the end of all my plight.

148. "Therefore, O Death, I beg you to descend,
since you are bound to heal my bitter days.
Pierce this my heart with your last, fatal blow,
for I, despite myself, my life abhor.
Until this hour I have despised your sight
but now I call you my most cherished friend.
Come to me, then, and break this heavy chain!
Come fast, and free me from this endless pain!"

149. Bitterly weeping after all these words,
he then recalled the almost fatal dart
his lovely nymph had hurled against his life,
and then the tender pity of her words
wherewith she told him to avoid the spear
that came against him whistling in the air—
oh, gentle words that made him now believe
that he should hope some mercy to achieve!

150. Weeping and sorely sighing on his bed,
our wretched youth in love desired to live
yet with his every cry called out for death.
Between this conflict of new hope and fear
the god of sleep out of his horrid doors
came to his room, and made him fall asleep.
So wan and weary had now grown our lad,
he heavily collapsed upon his bed.

151. But in the meantime his resourceful mother
 had gathered a large quantity of herbs
 to make a bath with which she hoped to cure
 the pain she thought her son felt in his side.
 For how was she to know that something else
 was causing all that anguish and lament?
 While she was readying her medicine,
 her husband, Girafone, entered in.

152. He asked at once about his dearest son,
 if he had come, that day, back from the wood.
 His woman (Alimena was her name)
 told him that he was home, and added soon
 that he had found her words so wearisome
 that she had better leave the lad alone,
 and let him sleep. "Therefore, I think it's best,"
 she said, "not to go up, and let him rest.

153. "I have prepared what's best for such a pain—
 a most effective bath, I do believe.
 When he has rested as his heart desires,
 I'll bathe all of his body with this thing.
 This is a bath that eases every pain,
 and will completely heal him everywhere.
 But let him rest as long as he desire,
 for, when he talks, his pain grows so much higher."

154. Yet his paternal love would not allow
 that he should not see Africo at once.
 Hearing his woman telling all those things,
 he felt a great unrest within his heart,
 and soon he walked into the little room
 where his dear boy lay sleeping in his bed.
 But fast asleep his ailing son he found,
 and so he covered him, and made no sound.

155. Back to his wife, he said, "My dear, our son
seems to be soundly sleeping in his bed.
So peacefully he's resting, it would be
indeed a sin to wake him up right now,
and I might even have brought back his pain
had I aroused him from his needed sleep.
"That's very true," his Alimena said;
"Disturb him not, and let him rest instead!"

156. For a long time Sleep held Africo bound
and fastened in his most relentless grip;
but when he finally relieved his breast,
heaving a bitter sigh, at last he woke.
Seeing himself unnoticed and alone,
back to his grief with all his thoughts he went,
for in his heart and mind could never die
the fair, sweet glance he had been wounded by.

157. But not to have the matter fully known
to his own father, who already knew,
pretending to be cured, he soon arose,
hiding the love that pricked him harshly still.
Thus more than once his head, his handsome face,
his cheeks and eyes he wiped with the bed sheet,
so wet and soaked for his nocturnal crying;
finally, he went out, perturbed, and sighing.

158. When he caught sight of his beloved son,
old Girafone hastened to inquire
about his sudden pain, and how he felt;
and, looking at him, Alimena, too,
asked the same question of her darling son.
He answered her, "My pain is almost gone;
as I awoke this morning—Mother, guess!—
the pain was gone, that gave me such distress."

159. The steaming bath was nonetheless prepared—
    so Girafone wished—for Africo.
    And he complied, to prove that nothing else
    was ailing him thus causing his distress.
    You are a bad physician, Girafone,
    for a hot bath can never heal the wound
    inclement Love makes quickly with his dart:
    you cannot see it in your son's deep heart.

160. But let it go at that. After the bath,
    Africo passed that day in great dismay,
    and so the next, and then another, too,
    and then another with no rest or peace.
    Unmindful of past happiness and joy,
    in melancholy and lament he lay,
    unable to remove his thoughts away
    from her who kept him moaning night and day.

161. Father, and mother, and his daily tasks
    he seemed no more to care for or recall.
    Nothing on earth was there for him to do,
    and nothing, nothing mattered any more.
    His every thought went only to the nymph
    who kept him in so dark a dungeon still.
    'Twas she who made his faintest hope so dear,
    and she alone who so renewed his fear.

162. Whenever to some corner he could go
    where no one noticed his unhappiness,
    there he would vent all of his flaming smart,
    blaming almighty Love for all his grief.
    This was his sole diversion, his one joy—
    to be alone and free to weep and wail,
    and, utterly unseen now and unheard,
    recall the things of love that had occurred.

163. Deep once again in his complaining mood,
Africo felt his wretchedness increase.
So weary had his torment rendered him
that he had lost all of his strength and zest.
Unwillingly, he lived day after day,
for Love's relentless chains had bound him so
that, caring but for death, he hardly ate—
which surely worsened his now hopeless state.

164. The healthy, rosy hue had fled his face,
his handsome face, so lean now and so gaunt.
His pallor was too manifestly sad;
his deeply sunken eyes too keenly stared.
Suffering had disguised his looks so much
that he could scarcely have been recognized.
He was no more the lad he used to be
when from the flames of Love he still was free.

165. And in what fashion could I ever tell
how sorely grieved his pitying father felt?
With words he often tried to comfort him,
saying, "My son, what is it pains you so,
what is it makes you so distressed and sad?
Oh, speak to me, and I do swear and say
that, if there's something any man can do,
I promise I will do it now for you.

166. "If it is something that cannot be gained
either through human intellect or might,
some other way we'll find, some other means
to root this wicked ill out of your life.
I want to see you healed of your unrest,
I want to see you healthy once again.
Some good advice, O my dear son, some cure
we'll find for what is ailing you, I'm sure."

167. In the same manner, his beloved mother
often approached him, asking what had made
his life so sad and so disconsolate,
and what had brought such anguish on his heart.
"Son, O my son," she said, "this pain you feel
distresses me so deeply that I think
I'm on the verge of madness. Every day
I see you go from bad to worse, I say."

168. What could poor Africo reply to this?
He only answered that his pain was gone,
but did not know why still he felt so ill.
Hoping that they may bother him no more,
at times, to please them, he would soon admit
it maybe was a headache ailed him so.
Thus he was given medicine and care,
but not for the real illness that was there.

169. Long having lived in such a woeful way,
Africo walked, one day, behind his flock,
slowly and slowly moving here and there,
and thinking only of his Mensola—
the maiden who tormented him so much—
when suddenly and unexpectedly
he saw a lovely fountain very near,
than a bright star more luminous and clear.

170. It was encircled all about with trees
and verdant boughs that cast a lovely shade
upon it. For a while he looked at it,
and then sat down upon its very edge,
musing on the misfortunes of his life
brought to so sad an end by ruthless Love.
Gazing on his reflection, he could trace
the wrinkles and the darkness of his face.

171. Ah, he felt pity, pity for himself,
  seeing his features so worn out and wan.
  No longer could he now control his tears,
  but loudly he began to weep and moan,
  cursing whatever happened on that day
  when he first met his nymph and fell in love,
  and saying, "To what grief and martyrdom
  my desperate existence had to come!"

172. Languorous, lost, his cheeks upon his hands,
  his elbows feebly resting on his knees,
  he wept, and in his tears these words he said,
  "O wretched me! What horrid life this is!
  Like snow in the warm sun it melts away,
  such is the grief that overwhelms my days.
  Ah, like dry wood in a great fire I burn,
  and no salvation can I yet discern.

173. "How much I love, and cannot fail to love,
  this cruel maiden that has won my heart!
  How much I want her, her alone I want
  above all things! And yet full well I see
  how in this bondage only grief I find,
  and how this flame that burns me day and night
  grants me no hope of ever going free
  unless the gift of death comes soon to me."

174. He looked about, and saw his handsome cows,
  his sleek, young bullocks play among themselves:
  each made the other happy with his love,
  and each was seen to answer with a kiss.
  He heard the birds rejoice with happy songs,
  finding each other with a loving call:
  he saw them rapt in their desirous flight,
  fulfilling all their longing and delight.

175. At this, Africo whispered to himself,
"O happy birds, how happier than I,
how dearer to great Venus you must be!
How merrier than mine your life appears!
How pleasanter your bliss than I can guess!
How much more gratitude, indeed, you owe
for the sweet fullness of delight and pleasure
Love lavishes upon you without measure.

176. "You sing, and are made happy by your song;
you make your merriment forever known,
whereas I weep in sadness and in woe,
and day and night destroy myself in grief.
Ah, all this weeping leads me but to death,
death that alone will free me from my pain,
without the smallest taste of any bliss
from her who made my spirit come to this."

177. Heaving another agonizing sigh,
poor Africo began to weep anew;
and so abundantly his tears outpoured
that they indeed resembled a small rill
flowing from both his cheeks down to his breast.
Oh, in the midst of all his misery,
down in the lovely fountain he could look
and talk to his own image in the brook.

178. Long his reflected image he addressed
till for his tears the fountain overbrimmed.
And long had he in futile fancies lain
until a new thought flashing in his mind
suddenly caused his weeping to decrease,
and somewhat made his grievous pain abate.
Recalling what from Venus he had heard,
he could not doubt that she would keep her word.

179. But seeing that such promise until now
 had not been kept, and seeing then himself
 so wretched that his death now seemed so near,
 he moaned, "It may be Venus has forgotten
 my misery and horrid agony,
 or does not see that death is all my gain."
 Therefore, he thought his sacrifice would bind her
 to her old promise, or at least remind her.

180. He rose, and to a corner quickly walked
 from where he saw the clear and ample sky.
 With tinder, there, and with his wonted skill
 he lighted up a bright and smokeless fire;
 then with a knife he cut and opened wide
 several twigs with which to feed the flame:
 a sweet, young lamb he saw and picked out then,
 the fairest and the fattest of the pen.

181. He seized it, brought it near the burning fire,
 held it between his legs and, knowing well
 the very thing to do, with a sharp blade
 he slew it, with a wound deep in its throat.
 Little by little, all its blood came out,
 and all of it he sprinkled on the flames;
 then the dead lamb he cut and split in two,
 and the two halves upon the fire he threw.

182. He sacrificed one half for Mensola,
 and made the other burn in his own name
 to see, should a quick miracle occur,
 if he was still to cling to some faint hope.
 Whatever the results, he soon would know
 whether it still was best not to despair.
 Pressing the barren plainland with his knee,
 he lifted up to Venus such a plea:

183. "O holy Goddess, whose great strength and worth
surpass all might in heaven and on earth;
O lovely Venus, mother of sweet Love,
who wounds each heart and saddens every soul,
with reverent heart I'm turning now to you,
the one and only one who rules men's lives:
O powerful and holy Goddess, deign
to hear me, so my prayer be not in vain.

184. "O Goddess, you know well with what great ease
I let myself be vanquished by your son
the day I saw Diana at the stream
together with the fair and festive band
of pretty nymphs; and how immediately
I felt your cruel arrow in my heart
for one of them, who was so sweet and fair
she was forever this my heart to share.

185. "And what sad woes have ever since been mine,
and what discomfort, suffering, and grief
I have until this moment known for her,
you clearly see far more than I can tell.
You also know that fortune until now
has been so hostile to me, that the groves
of all this valley witnesses can be,
which I have filled with tears of agony.

186. "My very face can tell you—look at me—
how all my life has been, and still will be,
an open conflagration of true love
until my death delivers me from woe.
Only your heavenly might can free me now
from all the sorrows you have made me know,
for if you still refuse to ease my pain,
death, death alone will loose me from this chain.

187. "'Twas you who caused my anguish to begin,
and you who, coming to me in my dream
together with your son, made me believe
that I should follow your divine advice.
You also promised, as you well recall,
that, most undoubtedly and in no time,
you'd give me my reward and make me glad:
instead, you left me wounded on my bed.

188. "It was your word revived my fainting hope,
and so, with faith in you, I soon resolved
to love forever that sweet nymph alone.
And then, one day, I saw her, she saw me,
but so afraid she at that moment grew
that she began to flee so fast away,
so mercilessly fast, no arrows go
with such a speed from their relentless bow.

189. "In vain with every praise and every prayer
did I attempt to make her wait for me:
as nimble as a hound away she fled,
showing too clearly and without a doubt
that she cared very little for my life.
And when she saw that in my new pursuit
I'd put all of my strength, with faultless art
at me she hurled a nearly fatal dart.

190. "O Goddess, you yourself could plainly see
that I would have been slain by such a blow
had it not been for a propitious tree
standing between her anger and my fate.
She leapt across the hill and disappeared,
leaving me lost and lonely down below,
and never more have I her beauty seen,
and always in deep anguish have I been.

191. "Therefore, O Goddess, I entreat you now
with all the prayers all human hearts can raise,
oh, bend a little your sweet glance on me,
and look with mercy on my bitter life.
Tenderly, send your son, and bid him dwell
in Mensola's cold heart, so that, if Love
enters her life and conquers it, she, too,
may know the flaming torture I go through.

192. "And if this favor you refuse to do,
oh, grant me this at least—that when my light
comes to its end (so greatly and so long
have I endured this agony and grief
that little time is left for me to go,)
may my beloved know of my sad death,
and, though my life displeased her so, at least
may not my end be greeted as a feast."

193. No sooner had this plea reached Venus' ear
than, gazing at the fire that burned before him,
Africo saw all twigs already spent,
and his long-dead lamb rise straight from the flames,
its two halves joined together once again:
once more alive, it bleated loud anew,
stood up a moment, burning not at all,
and then into the fire was seen to fall.

194. Africo had been weeping bitterly,
but this great miracle relieved his ache,
for it now seemed most evident to him
that the devout ascending of his plea
had moved to pity Venus in the sky.
Many and many a time he thanked the Goddess,
whose prodigy seemed clearly to portend
that all his misery was soon to end.

195. The sun was setting in the west already,
where but a fading gleam could now be seen.
Africo drew together all his flock
and drove it homeward for the coming night.
At home, at once his ruddy, radiant face,
so unexpectedly and gladly new,
caught the attention of his welcoming father,
and brought relief and solace to his mother.

196. There, when the stars were visible and bright
high in the sky, and night was everywhere,
the three of them ate supper, and began
to talk of what had happened in the day.
But, little caring for that idle chat,
and feeling in the kitchen ill at ease,
Africo rose and went, alone, to bed,
his soul with new and hopeful fancies fed.

197. Yet before slumber came to drowse his soul,
and finally enabled him to sleep,
numberless times, I think, he tossed and turned
upon his bed, and tossed and turned once more,
thus showing how his heart was set upon
his Mensola alone who pained him so:
but there was hope now in his mind although
one thought said "yes" and one retorted "no."

198. Finally, with the dawn about to break,
sleep came to close our hapless lover's eyes.
Lying upon his back, he lightly slept
when Goddess Venus stood before him, bright.
She carried in her arms her little child—
Love, fully armed with bow and darts and wrath.
The goddess came to stand right where he lay,
and in this fashion seemed to speak and say:

199. "The fervent plea and pious sacrifice
you offered to my throne have touched my heart.
Therefore, I will reward you lavishly
by granting everything your heart desires.
So rest assured, and let your faith be firm,
that all my power will henceforth be employed
to aid you, and, with it, that of my son,
if all, according to my will, is done.

200. "First, you must find a gown such as I say:
a wide and long one, falling at your feet,
exactly such as every maiden wears.
Take, then, a bow, an arrow, and go out,
perfectly looking like a gentle nymph,
in search of Mensola from hill to hill.
But this you must remember: you must seem
one of the nymphs, and walk, disguised, with them.

201. "Finally, when you find your Mensola,
quickly engage her in a pleasant talk
about such holy things as gods above,
and, listening and speaking, stay with her.
And so that you may know the thing to do,
I'll leave this darling child within your heart,
and he will teach you what she cares to hear—
words that will sound most beautiful and dear.

202. "When the right moment comes, and not before,
disclose your true identity to her.
She'll flee in terror like a frightened bird
chased by a falcon through the forest deep;
but see that, when you tell her who you are,
you're not so foolish as to let her be
faster in fleeing from your arms away
than you must be in forcing her to stay.

203. "And do not be afraid to use your strength,
for this my child will wound her in such way
she won't be able to escape your clutch
till you fulfill your wishes on her breast.
If faithfully you follow my advice,
you will accomplish all that you desire."
She vanished, but already in the east
the day dawned bright, and Africo got dressed.

204. It was an easy thing to understand
the meaning of this vision and this dream,
and so he gladly cherished her advice.
So high the burning flames leapt in his heart,
rekindled and revived by such new hope,
they overcame and seized his every sense.
And now his only thought, his only care
was how to find the dress he had to wear.

205. After much thought, he finally recalled
his mother had a very pretty gown
which he had seen her very seldom use.
"If I can steal it," to himself he said,
"it is the thing I need." He waited then
until he saw his mother leave the house:
that dress he had to fetch and safely hide
where he would find it when he should decide.

206. Luck favored him and smiled upon his plan,
for when the luster of the moon was spent
and the last lingering star consumed its light,
in the faint glimmer of the coming day
old Girafone rose and left his room,
eager to start his early work outside:
and there he was already at his chores
when his wife, also, quickly came outdoors.

207. On seeing both his parents in the field,
Africo grabbed his chance with no delay.
He went fast to a closet, opened it,
and found that gown after an easy search.
Well he accomplished what he wanted most,
for, being seen by none, he brought that dress
to a spot, a little distance from the house,
that never would the least suspicion rouse.

208. On his way home, he thought he had so far
completely followed the divine advice,
but his decision was he should not start
his search of Mensola that very day.
There, in the house, he found a fine-wrought bow;
also, a quiver wholly filled with darts.
Now everything was ready. That day went,
and rose another in the firmament.

209. Already Phoebus with his nimble steeds
had set the Lion's eastern tail ablaze;
already golden, every mountain peak
was seen to tower above the russet west;
but there were valleys still untouched and dark
when, rising early, Africo got hold
of bow and quiver, walked outside, and said,
"I'm going hunting, Mother," and he sped.

210. Straight to the spot he went where he had hidden
his mother's needed dress the day before.
There he at once removed all of his clothes,
and put, instead, that odd new garment on.
He bound a shoot of clematis about him
so as to walk with greater ease and speed.
Surely sweet Venus helped him, there with him,
so wonderful he looked, and neat and trim!

211. As yet uncombed, his hair was hanging down,
oh, not as long as woman's hair should be,
yet of such fairness it seemed spun of gold,
and of such curls in which all beauty beamed.
Alas, it was the anguish of his past
that spread a pallid hue upon his face;
but, luckily, his pallor now was such,
a maiden he resembled very much.

212. So thoroughly disguised as he was now,
he fastened, soon, his quiver to his right,
and grasped a weightless arrow and the bow.
Puzzled, he looked, then, at himself awhile,
and what he'd always been he was no more,
for, not a man, he seemed a woman now,
and those who of his trick were not aware
saw not a lad—a lady standing there.

213. In the same place he then concealed his clothes
where he had hidden and then found his dress.
Thus, in his new array, he started out,
quite slowly, toward the hills of Fiesole.
Still in the plain, before he reached their height,
many a savage beast he met and slew.
He heard, as he stood on the tallest of
the three hills, someone scream and something move.

214. Looking in the direction of that sound,
Africo saw a group of hunting nymphs,
pointing to him, and shouting all the while,
"Stay where you are! Wait for the beast to pass!"
Africo looked and wondered; then he saw
a fiercely wild and wildly roaring boar
with countless arrows sticking from its back.
From his bone-carved bow suddenly—oh, look!—

215. Africo let a faultless arrow go:
it pierced the wild boar's breast and stopped its heart,
despite the callous roughness of its hide:
the wounded animal now roared no more,
heavily falling down upon the ground.
It was the will of Venus and of Love
that Mensola should see it; right before
her eyes, fell, huge and dead, the wicked boar.

216. She called, and bade more nymphs come where she stood,
convinced that Africo was one of them.
When a fair crowd of nymphs was gathered there,
Mensola spoke, and told her lovely friends
of what she had just seen with her own eyes:
"I saw it: it was she who struck him dead.
What aim! Oh, never in my life had I
seen such a blow until this nymph came by."

217. I could not tell you what delight and bliss
Africo felt, that moment, in his heart,
hearing himself so greatly praised by one
who once had greatly shunned his very sight;
but only those can fully understand
who, too, have felt the wicked might of Love.
To those who still cannot, I say and swear
Africo almost grabbed her then and there.

218. But it was fear restrained him, only fear
of her companions and their handy bows.
After a while he felt at ease among them,
and said and answered what they cared to hear.
They all conversed, and he along with them,
about the fate of the wild boar now dead,
and how each nymph could recognize and count
the wounds she had inflicted in the hunt.

219. Mensola said, "Diana should be here:
oh, what a lovely present this would make!"
On hearing that the Goddess was not there,
Africo soon rejoiced within his heart.
Their conversation a long time revolved
around that strange and terrifying beast.
At last, they set a target up in view,
and, practising, their darts at it they threw.

220. Bending of bows and hurling of fast arrows
sharpened their courage and improved their aim.
It was Mensola's turn: she threw her dart,
and landed it much closer to the mark
than all her friends had done. Amazed and glad,
Africo grabbed his bow and placed his spear
so close to Mensola's that, all could see,
two were the winners—Mensola and he.

221. Love, who knows always what is best to make
two people fall in love, if so he will,
that day, resorted to his greatest art,
for not with words—with deeds he wished to bring
all of his plan to a delightful end.
Therefore, that morning, he behaved so well,
Mensola's arrows and then Africo's
landed together and were ever close.

222. Mensola, seeing that for every shot
she had once more to share her victory,
with ever-growing fondness looked at him,
her heart already burning with great love.
His gaze steadily fixed on her alone,
Africo seemed to please her more and more,
for he agreed with everything she said,
and, when he spoke, she nodded, also glad.

223. They spent some time in throwing darts and darts
 till they grew weary of their shooting game;
 therefore, they left that place, and all together
 went to a cavern not too far away.
 One of the nymphs began to build a fire,
 and on its burning flame that quickly rose
 some of the boar she roasted very slow,
 with other kinds of meats I do not know.

224. The sun already had resolved one third
 its wonted course when now the famished nymphs
 gathered together in the lovely shade
 cast there by a gigantic laurel tree.
 There on a massive stone they served the meat,
 perfectly roasted, with no gravy on;
 and chestnut bread they used to bake and eat,
 still unfamiliar with flour of wheat.

225. Their drink was water boiled with herbs and honey,
 and that to all of them was known as wine.
 The vessels that they drank from at that time,
 both large and small, were only made of wood.
 Assembling there, the whole fair throng of nymphs
 sat down and ate with relish and delight.
 Next to his Mensola, around the rock,
 Africo sat, and gladly heard and spoke.

226. At the conclusion of their merry meal,
 all of the nymphs arose and, sweetly singing,
 in the direction of the mountain went
 in lively groups of two, or three or four,
 as each one chose, to fill her heart's desire.
 Africo did not leave his Mensola:
 they walked together with three nymphs away
 along the mountain slope toward Fiesole.

227. As I have mentioned, Mensola had grown
so fond of Africo for the great skill
that he had shown in archery that day,
and for his bold appearance and sweet speech,
that she already loved him more than life,
and now could only crave his happy sight.
But do not think that ever in her mind
she lodged one thought immodest or unkind.

228. She only knew, and firmly was convinced,
Africo was a nymph from out of town,
for not one sign of manliness was there
to make her think that he was not a lass.
Certainly, had she known what she knew not,
she would have been less quick in praising him,
or showing, with the others, all her charm:
instead, she would have shamed him with great harm.

229. How deeply and how much Africo loved her,
there is no need to tell: I've said enough.
But as they went together in this way,
the fire he kept hidden in his breast
began to burn more hastily than wax.
Oh, there he was, so close to his delight,
able to touch her, praise her, speak and hear:
his heart was beating fast with love and fear.

230. And to himself he thought, "What must I do?
I don't know what to say or how to act.
If I reveal my longing to her now,
I am afraid I may displease her so
that all her love will turn to hate at once,
and she with all her friends will hunt me down.
But if I do not act this very day,
another chance may never come my way.

231. "If only these three nymphs still here with us
would go away! I would be then alone,
alone with my sweet Mensola at last,
and could more safely finally disclose
myself to her and who I truly am.
Then, if she tried to run, I'd be so quick
to grab and hold her that she would not flee
away from my embrace, away from me.

232. "But I'm afraid that they will stay with us
throughout the day, and never leave us free.
Ah, if I do not act immediately,
never again will such a chance be mine.
Better to grab a little bliss today
than still to wait for what may never be!"
At this, his nymph he would have quickly seized,
but then did not dare touch her in the least.

233. "Now help me, Venus! Teach me what to do;
now, now, oh, give me now your dear advice.
It seems to me that the right hour has come
when I must hold her in my fond embrace."
But then he thought awhile, and changed his mind,
lest he should run the risk of ruining all.
Meanwhile the flames of love burned more and
    more,
and fear and fondness waged their fiercest war.

234. The other nymphs in the meantime had gone
adown the hill, and were already near
the valley where the two tall mountains split.
Right there Love chose to grant Africo's wish,
determined not to wait another day
to bring about his happiness at last.
They were still going happily together
when down below they heard the sound of water.

235. They walked in that direction a short while
when they perceived two fully naked nymphs,
gracefully bathing in the lovely pool
right at the place where the two mountains met.
When they arrived, they lifted up their skirts,
and, their feet braving the cool-flowing waves,
they asked the others, saying more or less,
"Oh, what do you suggest? Shall we undress?"

236. It was the hottest hour of the day,
and surely those cool waters lured them all
into their bland refreshment instantly.
Knowing themselves to be quite safe from harm,
and seeing then the pool so clear and pure,
they did at last as they had thought and said.
So while each nymph was getting quick undressed,
sweet Mensola young Africo addressed,

237. saying, "O my dear friend, why don't you stay,
and bathe here with the rest of us awhile?"
Africo answered in a resonant voice,
"Dear friends, I'll do whatever you suggest,
for anything you wish is my delight."
But this he whispered, talking to himself,
"I shall be forced, if they remove their dress,
at last my great desire to confess."

238. He deemed it best to let them all disrobe
before he, too, decided to undress:
this way they would not wield their darts against him.
Slowly, he started stripping off his dress,
thinking that, once he stepped into the pool
to bathe like them, they all would scatter fast,
in terror and in shame, while, brave and bold,
Mensola he at last would seize and hold.

239. Slowly he was disrobing, very slowly,
while now the nymphs were splashing in the waves.
All naked, suddenly he turned to them,
thus baring everything he had in front.
Suddenly startled, all the nymphs at once
uttered a sigh of helplessness and fear.
"Good heavens! Oh, good heavens!" they began
to scream, most frantic. "She's a man—a man!"

240. The same thing happens when a hungry wolf
suddenly breaks into a flock of lambs:
he seizes one of them and steals away,
leaving the others fleeing and afraid:
bleating and bleating in confusion, lost,
the little creatures try to save their lives;
thus Africo, now running through those waters,
grabbed the one nymph he liked more than the others.

241. Dismayed, the others from the water sped,
frantically looking for their scattered gowns;
but none of them was given time to dress.
Shielding as best they could their nakedness,
and with no thought of waiting for each other,
they fled and fled, and never turned to look:
some went this way and some the other way,
and on the bank all of their weapons lay.

242. But in the water Africo was clasping
Mensola in his arms, despite her tears.
With kisses, kisses on her virgin face
he kept repeating such sweet words to her,
"Life of my life, my darling, do not cry
if I have seized you. Goddess Venus herself
has promised you to me, my life, my love:
oh, weep no more, for all the gods above!"

243. Mensola did not listen to his plea,
but with her strength, with all her strength she fought
to free herself and run from his embrace:
now this way and now that, most violently
she shook, in vain, in his relentless arms
while tears of wrath, not love, streamed down her cheeks.
But futile was her fight, for Africo,
holding her in his grip, did not let go.

244. Throughout this lively struggle in the pool,
someone who until now had sadly slept
lifted his head with soon-awakened pride,
and started knocking, wrathful, on the door.
With such a rage he pushed his head inside
that not with peace he entered but with war:
indeed, a roaring battle, fierce and loud,
with even, perhaps, the shedding of some blood.

245. But when at last Sir Stock had won Black Hill
and stepped into the castle joyously,
the foe that had resisted his advance
welcomed and greeted him with great content.
Finally, having labored long and hard
to leave the conquered post in perfect peace,
he shed a pitying tear, and left the castle
meek as a lamb, and wholly dumb and docile.

246. Mensola, seeing that her maidenhood
had now against her will been snatched away,
turning to Africo with bitter tears,
said, "Now that you've fulfilled your every wish,
deceiving thus a foolish girl like me,
let us at least get off the stream: my grief
is such that to this world I'll say goodbye:
right now, of my own hand I want to die."

247. Africo, hearing all these anguished words,
to please her, left the stream along with her.
Her desolation and her deep-felt ache
resounded with great sorrow in his heart.
His longing now had somewhat been appeased,
and yet the flames of love deep in his breast
grew at this moment warmer, and leapt higher,
her grief and tears rekindling his desire.

248. After they both had dressed, with no delay
Mensola seized her dart and, with no word,
pointed the cruel steel against her breast
to end her life; but Africo, at once,
reading the dismal darkness of her thought,
rushed where she was, and grabbed her by the arm:
into the woods he threw her dart away,
and then with tenderness began to say:

249. "For heaven's sake, what did you try to do?
But why? Oh, why, my love? What foolishness!
How could you even have such horrid thought,
and bring yourself to such despair and fright?
My God! What would I do, poor wretched thing,
were I to lose your love and loveliness?
Another hour on earth I could not stand,
and I would take my life with my own hand."

250. Mensola felt such pain now in her heart,
oh, so much pain, that she collapsed and swooned
in Africo's supporting arms at once.
He gazed upon the beauty of her face,
unable to restrain his tears: he feared
that death had come to steal her life away.
Carrying her, in great bewilderment,
to hide beneath some sheltering trees he went.

251. He laid her down, and sat beside her; then,
holding her lovely frame in his left arm,
he wiped her tear-stained cheeks with his right
   hand.
And, weeping, weeping in his great lament,
with tenderness and bitterness he said:
"Death, now you have what you have wanted most;
but since my very life and joy you stole,
I, too, must be together with her soul."

252. Kissing the deadly pallor of her face,
and calling her, and calling her, he said,
"My love, my love, oh, why has cruel fate,
and this sad day divided us so soon?"
And looking at her still, these things and more
he said, accusing, cursing his desire
for running to its pleasure in such haste,
and hurting Mensola, so dear and chaste.

253. Long had he wept, and long bemoaned his fate
over the deadly pallor of her face;
a thousand times and more, with endless woe,
had he with kisses wiped her tears away,
when, as he was about to end his life—
for death alone seemed his salvation now,
so weary of still living had he grown—
he heard Mensola sigh and feebly moan.

254. A long, long time in the thin, empty air
Mensola's spirits wandered, loose and free,
before to her fair body they returned,
resuming their own places once again.
When she, at last, came to her senses, soon,
heaving a sigh, bewildered, terrified,
she moaned, "Unhappy me! I'm dying, dying,"
and, uncontrolled, once more she started crying.

255. Seeing his Mensola alive, alive,
whom he had thought until this moment dead,
Africo felt his heart leap up with joy,
and with these words began to comfort her:
"O my so fresh and fragrant, happy rose,
that give all of this torment to my life,
oh, do not cry, my love, oh, do not be
afraid, for you are safe right here with me.

256. "Look, you are in the arms of one who loves you
more than the world, and only wants your joy.
Your every grief, your every ill and ache
are the one saddest anguish of my heart.
My God! My God! A while ago I feared
that death had come to bind you with its chain,
and so I thought I, too, like you, should die
when, thanks to God above, I heard you sigh."

257. "Poor me! Poor me! Poor, helpless, helpless girl!"
Mensola cried, looking at Africo.
"Why was I born? Oh, why was I to live
such wretched life?" she said in all her tears.
"Better it would have been, had I been strangled
right in my cradle! Or, the very day
that I was told to wear Diana's dress
a savage boar had gored me, merciless!"

258. "Comfort yourself, my love, my lovely soul,"
Africo answered, "for you break my heart
with all your melancholy and despair,
and with your thoughts that, shunning peace and
   rest,
make all your life so miserable be.
But there is now no need for such dismay,
for you are with the one who loves you more
than life, and you alone wants to adore.

259. "So that you may believe I love you so,
and that all I have said is good and true,
I want to tell you all that you should know.
Alone and carefree, four long months ago,
I happened to go hunting on this hill
when, at the threshold of a lovely wood,
voices I heard; so I began to walk
nearer and nearer, to make out who spoke.

260. "Sitting around a lovely fountain then,
many a nymph I saw, and, in their midst,
Goddess Diana higher than the rest:
with a stern sermon all unknown to me
she was then warning each and all of you.
Right at that moment I beheld your eyes,
and your great beauty wounded then my heart,
that very instant, with Love's sudden dart."

261. He also told her how he kept concealed
there a long time, merely to gaze at her,
and how he grew so fond of her alone
he could not sate or even take his glance
off the enchanted splendor of her face—
and, saying so, he kissed it once again—
and how, when "Mensola, let's go" he heard,
at last he knew her name, the sweetest word.

262. He then recounted all the tears and sighs
he had in great abundance known for her,
and all his suffering and sore distress.
He told how Venus on her word of honor
had promised her to him, still sound asleep,
and thus had made his hope reburgeon soon.
How many times he, then, renewed his quest!
And such details he made now manifest.

263. He told her how he found her then, one day,
all, all alone, and she began to flee;
he begged her, begged her not to run away,
yet she kept running, deaf to every plea.
She seized a dart and hurled it in mid-air,
but, long before it landed on an oak,
"Watch out!" she cried, and then she fled away,
and never could he see her since that day.

264. He told her of the offer he had made
to holy Venus, and of her reply,
and how, obeying her advice, in haste
he found a woman's dress, and, so disguised
as to resemble by all means a nymph,
he started out in search of her alone.
"Oh, then at last I found you on the hill;
and now what happened next you know full well.

265. "So I have told you all the smart and ache
I have endured and suffered for my love.
If I have seized you much against your will,
I did so only out of great despair,
and not to hurt you, dear, in any way.
Love made me do it, who for you alone
has kept me in such grief and such a flame:
so, not on me, on him lay all your blame."

266. Mensola heard and understood full well
what Africo had told her of his love—
how it was she who conquered first his heart,
and how Love made him, then, do what he did.
So, deep within her breast, a fire was lit,
that at this moment made her sweetly sigh.
Love had already wounded a stern maid,
though still she thought herself by Love betrayed.

267. "Alas," she said, "I do remember well—
I was pursued by someone long ago,
a long, long way. Now whether it was you,
who've so dishonored me, I cannot tell.
I only know that, to discourage him,
I turned, emboldened by my sudden wrath,
and hurled a dart at him from where I stood,
seeing myself still followed and pursued.

268. "And I recall (I wish it were not true!)
that, when I saw my dart against him go,
I don't know why, by sudden pity moved,
I cried out loud, 'Watch out! Watch out!' and soon
began to flee; but as I turned, I saw
my arrow split the oak on which it fell;
then in the wood I found my hiding-place.
If you're that man, I had not seen your face.

269. "In all the days I've been Diana's nymph,
never, oh, never have I seen a man,
and I would be most grateful to the gods
if you had never set your eyes on me.
For I would still be numbered in the throng
of those who heed Diana's holy law,
whereas, poor me, I soon will be thrown out,
and even lose my life, beyond a doubt.

270. "But you, young man, the cause of all my grief,
and even, I am certain, of my death,
though, as I told you, I am not to blame,
you will live on with total unconcern.
Let trees and beasts, who saw what happened here,
tell our Diana nothing but the truth—
that I did try to fight your violence,
but that you overwhelmed my every sense.

271. "A pure and innocent young maiden, I
have been the victim of your vile deceit.
But of this sin I will absolve myself
by taking now my life with my own hands.
When, wretched me! I will no longer be
in this unhappy world so full of ill,
you will enjoy your triumph, ever free,
without the slightest care for hapless me."

272. Africo held her tightly on his breast,
saying in all his tears, "Unhappy me!
Don't think that I could leave you all alone,
my darling love, my life, my everything!
Instead, for my love's sake, oh, promise me
to banish from your mind this horrid thought.
For, long, oh, long before you meet your death,
I will precede you out of this sad earth.

273. "How could I ever live away from you,
my love, my dearest love?" At this, he kissed
her sweetest lips and her angelic face,
and with his hand he wiped her lovely eyes,
saying, "You have been made in paradise—
how true, how true," and, smoothing then her curls,
he added, "I have never seen such hair,
so silken and so golden and so fair.

274. "Oh, blessed be the year, the month, the day,
the time, the hour, and the sweet season, too,
when this enchanting face was made above,
with all the rest of you, and rightly so!
If I began to search through all the world,
and then inside the legions of the sky,
among the goddesses I'd never view
a girl that might compare, my love, with you.

275. "You are the lively fountain of all grace,
the limpid light of every gracefulness.
You are so simple, so naïve and true,
you are the only one whose soul shines bright
with every virtue, every courtesy.
You are the only guidance of my life;
you are so soft and delicate and dear
that all the beauty of the world is here.

276. "Therefore, I beg you, Mensola, my love,
don't ruin such a great and lovely thing—
for this, indeed, you are—with your sad thoughts
or any other deed of wickedness.
Chase all this mournful madness from your mind,
and don't be angry with me any more.
What has been done we never can undo,
even if I should die right now with you.

277. "And so with all my heart I beg you, love,
be a wise girl, and worry not at all:
take what is best, and let the worst go by.
Comfort your frightened spirit, and, instead,
embrace me as I do, and hold me close,
and kiss me with your kisses of delight,
my darling love, as I kiss you, you see,
and take, you too, the same delight of me."

278. With all the sweetest words Africo spoke
Love bound Mensola's heart still more and more
until her grief had somewhat fled away,
and she agreed that what had been, had been.
The love that she had felt for Africo
when she believed he truly was a nymph
now was rekindled in her heart, and stirred
by the enchantment of his every word.

279. So, wishing to reward his love in part,
she threw an arm around his neck, but still
she did not want to please him with a kiss
lest she be deemed too easy to possess.
She said, "What shall I do, what shall I do?
There's nothing that can save me any more
if this atrocious deed, this horrid sin
is known by stern Diana, my great queen.

280. "No more will I, as I have always done,
go bathing in the stream with all the nymphs,
nor will I dare—my fate has so decreed—
wander where I may meet another friend,
for if but one should know what I have done,
she would accuse me to our Goddess soon.
So I must live alone at any cost,
and shun the friends I used to cherish most.

281. "And I can see that, if I kill myself,
my sin will not be lessened by my death,
and that, had you not done the thing you did,
fate would have willed it, much against our wish.
If I believed the contrary of this,
I would not let tomorrow's sun be mine,
for truly I would have for such offence
already made commensurate amends.

282. "Your solace has so greatly soothed my heart
that I have altogether changed my mind.
Your tender words have so affected me
that all my cruel will is here no more.
But in all frankness let me tell you now
that I can never let you stay with me,
as you desire, for this indeed would mean
sin over sin; besides, we would be seen.

283. "You would be recognized by all those nymphs
who were with me and saw you here today.
And if they recognized you, you perhaps
would soon be killed by them, and, if not that,
you'd make them know the thing they know not yet.
Believe me, if they ever see me here,
I'll say to them that everything went right,
it was not you but I who won the fight.

284. "But I will do my utmost from this day
to shun, if possible, their company.
And now that you have taken from my life
what I'll be never able to regain,
young man, I beg you, leave me with my grief;
leave me alone, and I will do my best
to go about my chores and be resigned.
Oh, if you love me, go away! Be kind!"

285. Indeed, the very nature of her words
had made Africo know that in her heart
Love had already kindled his great fire,
but that she was still bashful and still coy.
Therefore, aware of all she meant to say,
he thought, "Before I leave this happy place,
I will, sweet maiden, make you so agree
that you must sing another song with me."

286. He kissed her once again, and said, "My love,
life of my life, O sweetest mouth of all,
O fresh, and lovely, and most radiant face—
the only solace of my great desire—
you, you alone are mistress of my life,
and you I love much more than God above.
I feel reborn now that you, too, as I,
take but the best and let the worst go by.

287. "How can I bear, my love, to see you go
if, loving you so dearly and so much,
I die whenever you are not with me?
For if I am with you, I cannot feign
a greater happiness upon this earth.
Oh, only Love knows well how, day and night,
I sigh for you, and nothing else can cheer me
if I don't see your lovely face still near me.

288. "And let us just suppose that I could leave,
as you suggest: how could I ever smile,
thinking of you, so sad and so forlorn,
and living in such grief because of me?
I might not even see you any more,
and this would give my days much more dismay
than I have had, and a much greater strife,
and make me long for death, no more for life.

289. "But since you will not let me stay with you
right here, then there is something you can do:
come with me to my house where you will stay
forever with my mother, if you wish.
And if you live with her, of this I'm sure,
not only she, but also my dear father,
will treat you as a daughter of their own
though as a daughter-in-law you will be known."

290. "Oh, never, never," Mensola replied,
"never will I set foot into your house,
where this my sin would suddenly be known
and I would have to live my life with you
and thus prolong my wickedness and guilt.
I'd rather die, I tell you, rather die
than go where people may suspect and see
that I have lost my dear virginity.

291. "I did not join Diana's holy throng
ever to go into the world again.
If I had wanted to spin wool at home
with my own mother, and become a bride,
I would be living three long miles away
with my dear father, who was fond of me,
and loved me more than life: five years, no less,
I have already worn Diana's dress.

292. "Therefore, I beg you—if my begging helps—
for all that love you have revealed to me,
for all that love that caused me so much harm,
oh, leave me, leave me, and go home alone.
And in the name of her who, as you say,
wounded your heart for me, I swear to you
that for your love alone I want to live,
and this my heart to you alone I give."

293. Africo now replied, "If I believed
that you would keep the promise you have made,
and that I'd be forever in your heart,
all of my fear would for a moment cease.
But what I dread and makes me suffer most
is that, if I now leave you here alone
in this deep wood, as soon as I am gone
I'll lose you: so this thing cannot be done."

294. Mensola said, "I will come often here,
to this same spot, and therefore more than once
you'll see me; more than once, if so you wish,
you'll talk to me with honesty of thought.
And, I assure you, I will keep my word
whenever you desire to visit me,
for I am half in love, as I believe,
and all my heart to you I wish to give."

295. Hearing these words and knowing what they meant,
Africo greatly in his heart rejoiced.
Full well he knew that Love, now burning low,
had banished every hatred from her mind.
He held her closer, closer in his arms,
and, kissing, kissing her angelic face,
added, "Now listen, dear, to what I say,
since you're determined all alone to stay.

296. "If you don't mind, my fresh, new-budded rose,
grant me a final grace before I go.
How dear your lovely body is to me,
and how I toiled to have it, you know well,
O star of my whole life; and yet you say
that I must leave, to prove my love to you.
So may it please you now to grant me this—
another little token of your bliss.

297. "With less displeasure I will go away
since you so wish that I must now depart.
Oh, tell me that you will, and I will do
something to thrill your heart as well as mine,
and then tomorrow I will here return
to see you once again, for you're the one
in whom all of my pleasure I have put:
oh, let me gather Love's delightful fruit!"

298. "Unhappy me! What more do you desire,"
Mensola said, "what other bliss and joy
can you still wish from this unlucky girl
than what you had already? Go, young man!
It's getting late, and you should not be here.
Please, go, and leave me, as I said, alone.
There is of daylight but a fainting trace:
people may come and find us in this place."

299. "You know full well that the delight I felt
when I was with you has not perished yet.
You know the joy that bound me to your breast:
but it was mingled with such grief and pain
that it was, truly, but a little bliss.
Now, only now that we have both made peace,
will new delight be more divine and sweet,
and our contentment fuller, more complete."

300. "Why do you ask me, O beloved youth,
to add new evil to the evil done?
Were I to act according to your wish,
how well I know that I would suffer more,
even if great Diana nothing knew.
So, as a gift to me, oh, leave at once,
I beg you once again: who knows—I'll grieve
more than you reckon when I see you leave."

301. "My love, my very soul," Africo said,
"what harm can come to you from what we did
if we are careful never to reveal it
to great Diana or to any man?
Oh, do not worry, for no grief will come
and no one will harass you. We shall be
so cautious that no one will ever know,
except perhaps for God, the thing we do.

302. "And rest assured that, if I go away
without another token of your grace,
I shall this very day die from my grief:
so show, my dear, some mercy on my life!"
Once more, once more he kissed her then and there,
saying, "Oh kiss me, kiss me, my sweet rose!
Do not be bashful, but have joy, instead,
and, if I love you, do not wish me dead!"

303. More flatteries and pleas than I can name
did Africo, that day, invent and say
to Mensola a hundred times and more,
kissing her mouth, her chin, and all her face,
so ardently that often she cried out
with a delicious cry of happiness.
And more and more he kissed her throat and breast,
which seemed with violets forever blest.

304. What tower so strongly raised above the ground
could ever stand, if buffeted and torn
by countless blows, and would not fall instead,
or bend, at least, beneath the hostile might?
What other cruel woman on this earth
would not have yielded to such ardent pleas
and to such kisses? Africo's great love
sufficed to bid the tallest mountain move.

305. Mensola's heart was not made out of steel:
therefore she stood half shaken and half won.
Unable to withstand Love's mighty blows,
she finally was conquered and enchained,
and, having had a taste of his delight
commingled with some injury and pain,
she even thought her suffering to be
the consequence of such sweet ecstasy.

306. Indeed, she was so innocent and pure,
she never could have thought that something new
would come of what had happened in the stream.
So chaste and pure was she, she did not know
by what occurrence and by what device
men are conceived and born upon this earth.
She did not know that Africo and she
could cause with their embrace such thing to be.

307. She kissed him, and she murmured, "O my friend,
I do not know what destiny or fate
wants me to grant whatever you desire,
compelling me to heed your every wish,
and fight no more. Therefore I yield to you,
a helpless girl unable to resist
Love and the winning power of his dart:
for you alone He came to wound my heart.

308. "So do with me, beloved, as you will,
for I am yours, and only yours to have.
My boldness and my courage I have lost
to fight the power of Love and of your plea.
But let me beg you, if you love me still:
when you have finished with me, leave at once,
lest any friend of mine should soon appear,
and find me in your company still here."

309. Africo, at these words, was overjoyed,
seeing his wish about to be fulfilled.
Kisses, and kisses, kisses once again
he gave her, waiting for his coming bliss.
Nature, not cunning, helped them at this point:
they lifted up their skirts, and suddenly
they seemed one person, and no longer two—
indeed, a natural thing for them to do.

310. They kissed and bit each other on the lips,
clasped in a strong embrace that could not end.
"My love! My love!" each to the other cried,
"Water, oh, water, for the fire is high!"
The millstone did its grinding, hard and fast,
while each was closer to the other still.
"Oh, hold me! Hold me more! Now stop, or I,
if you don't help me soon, will surely die."

311. The water came, and all the fire was quenched;
the millstone paused, and our two lovers sighed.
As God decreed and willed, Africo made,
right at that moment, Mensola become
pregnant with a most handsome baby boy,
so winsome and so worthy that, in time,
he far excelled all enemies and friends,
as I will tell before my story ends.

312. The day was nearly gone. There was a faint
trace of the sun still visible around
when, at the end of their ecstatic deed,
they still were savoring each other's sight.
Africo, who had promised to depart,
suddenly now grew sad and sorely grieved
while Mensola, still fast in his embrace,
felt his last kisses on her lovely face.

313. "Oh, be forever cursed, dark night," he said,
"for all your envy of our great delight.
Why do you bid me leave such loveliness
so quickly when you know as well as I
that I may never have such bliss again?"
With these, and with so many words of woe,
he told her all his love and all his sighing,
for leaving was to him far worse than dying.

314. Beautiful in her beaming bashfulness,
Mensola stood, unaware of her new sin,
and wondering why, to please her Africo,
the second time had been much easier.
It even seemed that what she now had done
was sweeter and devoid of any pain.
Yet she was still afraid lest she be caught
in error; so but this became her thought:

315. "I know of nothing more that I can do;
why, then, are you still hesitant to go?
Since you have had the joy you wanted most,
again I beg you, if you love me still:
oh, leave at once, and stay with me no more
so that no living soul may find us here.
Oh, please, believe me, safe I will not be
if you do not depart at once from me.

316. "Look, every leaf that stirs now makes me think
that my companions are already here.
Therefore, be good, and leave immediately,
else all the blame will fall on me alone.
Believe me, your departure grieves me, too,
and yet for our own good it has to be.
Besides, it's evening, and the night is near,
and we have miles and miles to go from here.

317. "But tell me now your name before you go,
that it may keep me company meanwhile.
I will remember it, and thus be sure
Love's heavy burden weighs upon me less."
Africo answered, "O my soul, my love,
how can I bear to live far from your eyes?"
To Mensola his name he mentioned then,
and kissed her, and was kissed, again, again.

318. Never could I recount how many times
our two young lovers were about to go.
Their kisses and their words could not be told
in all the thousand cantos of a book.
But every lover understands it well,
if once he tasted of the same delight:
he knows what grief, what suffering it is
to say goodbye to such ecstatic bliss.

319. And so, not once, a thousand times and more
they kissed each other: they would walk one step,
but soon would turn about and meet again
for still more tearful kisses on their lips.
"Why do I have to lose you, darling love?"
each to the other said with countless sighs.
They did not have the heart to go away:
they left, came back one minute more to stay.

320. But when they saw that they could not delay
their sorrowful departure any more,
clasped in each other's arms, for the last time
they kissed and kissed again, again, again,
with strength that nearly took their breath away,
so much had mighty Love united them.
For a long while in such embrace they were,
she clinging fast to him, and he to her.

321. Yet in the end they parted company.
But, before leaving, hand in hand they stood,
and, gazing then into each other's eyes,
they mentioned where they would soon meet again.
And so they bade their ultimate farewell
with great and endless anguish in their hearts:
"Oh, go with God, my Mensola, goodbye!"
"My Africo, God watch you from the sky!"

322. Africo then along the plainland went,
and Mensola began to climb the hill.
With dart in hand, in deep concern she walked,
bitterly sighing for her grievous sin.
Africo, still not far, still not too far,
pursued her with his glance and with his love,
turning around at every step he took
for one more glimpse of her, for one more look.

323. Mensola, too, with fondness often turned
to gaze at him she loved against her will,
at him who now had wounded so her heart
that no one else but he was her desire.
One at the other from a distance waved,
sending more greetings and one more farewell,
until each other they could see no more
for the thick forest stretching right before.

324. Africo went at once right to the place
where he that morning had concealed his clothes.
There he undressed in haste, and once again
resumed his manly garment of before.
Then he went home, pretending to be gay,
and, first of all, put back the stolen dress
where it belonged, so quickly that his mother
was none the wiser for it, nor his father.

325. Long had old Girafone and Alimena
awaited the return of their young son,
and long had they been watching down the path
to see if he was coming home at last.
So, when they saw their Africo return,
their hearts were overflowed with happiness,
and each of them began to ask, with great
love and affection, why he was so late.

326. With many lies and many more pretexts
Africo tried to hide his burning love,
which, to be truthful, now consumed his heart
much more than fire devours a layer of pitch.
But each excuse was worth less than a pea,
for he could only think, deep in his heart:
"Oh, will it be tomorrow? When, oh, when
shall I kiss that mouth, those beaming eyes again?"

327. Thus, musing, he remembered all the things
that he had done, recalling each detail,
and finding great delight in such sweet thoughts.
O happy recollections of the time
that they had spent together! O sweet hours!
It was quite late, and so he went to sleep.
But through the night no rest did he enjoy:
awake with all his memories he lay.

328. And now let's briefly turn to Mensola.
Alone and pensive, up the hill she went,
deeply repented of the wicked sin
she thought she had committed. She said often,
striking her forehead with remorseful hand,
"Since fate has brought such shame upon my life,
come, Death, to me, and hide my broken vow!
This final grace, oh grant me: kill me now!"

329. In such despair, she reached the mountain top,
and then crossed over to the eastern slope,
the side that, being first to face the sun,
is first to feel the luster of the day.
There was, that side the mountain, I believe,
no farther down than a quick dart would go,
a cavern hanging on the stream below,
which at that point far larger seemed to flow.

330. Once in the cave that was her dwelling-place,
all her perturbing thoughts beset her more,
and all her pain grew sharper in her breast.
"Poor me!" she sadly moaned, "Oh, why, oh, why,
the day Africo found my face so fair
around Diana's fountain, why, oh, why
did I not die? Why was I still alive
the hour (O curse!) I saw this lad arrive?

331. "Oh, God! And with what courage must I face
holy Diana now? I do not know
how to behave before her, what to do.
I only know that terror wears my life,
and freezes all my senses and my soul.
I feel a lump now rising in my throat,
for such is my distress, so great my smart,
bewilderment and war are in my heart.

332. "Come, O sweet Death, to this unhappy girl,
come to this worldly sinner. Come to me,
born to such evil fate, with no delay!
For at this moment you alone, O Death,
can gladden me by making me forget
my lost virginity. It is my heart
now tells me I will come to you, instead,
if you don't come to me, as I have said.

333. "Oh, my companions, you do not yet know
that I can be no longer in your midst.
Oh, dear, dear friends, who have until this day
shown such great love and tenderness to me!
I am no longer innocent and pure,
and you will track me like a hunted beast.
My wicked sin is written on my brow,
for I have broken our most holy vow.

334. "My story now resembles yours so much,
O poor Callisto, once a nymph like me,
and then by stern Diana hunted down
from place to place in everlasting woe.
But it was Jove betrayed you, as you know,
and yet she turned you into a wild bear.
You wandered then, and feared the hunter's bow,
able no more to speak but just to low.

335. "And you, nymph Cialla, once Diana's mate,
you by the Goddess, too, were struck and slain:
the day Mugnone seized you, you were killed
together with the man still in your arms.
And now you are a fountain, and Mugnone
flows at your foot and bathes the valley's edge.
Against my will I've joined your company.
Oh, curse upon this day! Oh, curse on me!

336. "I seem to feel my limbs now being turned
into a flowing river by Diana,
or maybe into a thick-coated beast,
or a bird ready to take flight and go,
or a tree showing all its boughs in bloom—
and, ah, no more the human form I was.
To bear a spear I am allowed no more,
nor to go hunting as I did before.

337. "Father! O mother! O brothers and sisters,
the day Diana took me from your arms,
and you put on me this religious gown,
I well remember that you ordered me
to give Diana and her faithful throng
my loyalty forever. To these hills
you led me then, oh, not that I might stain
my soul, but that a virgin I remain.

338. "You do not know that I have broken faith
with our most holy One, and therefore lie
in so much anguish. You cannot suspect
in what despair and grief my life now dwells.
And if you knew, no pity you would have,
no mercy on me. On the contrary,
I would immediately be slain by you—
and that would be the rightful thing to do."

339. So bitter was poor Mensola's lament,
so uncontrolled her grief, so sad and loud
her weeping, so heartrending her dismay,
I could not quite describe it on this page,
for every sigh and every sob would be
a hundred times more truthful than my word.
She would have made a stone, a rock, a tree
feel sorry for her endless misery.

340. With bitter lamentation and hot tears
she spent or, rather, wore the night away.
But when the day dawned beautiful and bright,
weary from all those long and sleepless hours,
she felt her tearful eyes at last grow numb.
Bereft of strength and all desire to live,
disconsolate, and lost, and sobbing still,
she fell asleep, so much against her will.

341. Africo, more than ever now in love,
and more than ever burning, fast arose
with the new morning, for but little sleep
had come to soothe his anguish in the night.
To the high hill he went and to the place
where he and Mensola, the day before,
had known so much delight and happiness,
the loss of which was now his sole distress.

342. Mensola should be there, he firmly hoped.
But when he failed to see her, so he thought,
"It is too early, far too early still."
And there he waited so that, when she came,
she'd find him at the spot agreed upon.
To make his waiting somewhat seem less long
a lovely garland he began to bind
with large and little buds of every kind.

343. After he made and finished his first wreath,
    he placed it on his blond hair as a crown.
    Then he began a second one, for which
    he chose far better blossoms, mixing them
    with leaves of fragrant and most tender herbs.
    He said, "When she arrives, with these my hands
    on Mensola's fair tresses I'll put this,
    and then I'll greet her with a loving kiss."

344. In vain, our youth kept waiting, waiting there,
    for his dear Mensola was still asleep.
    To make his waiting somewhat seem less hard,
    he picked more flowers for his own delight,
    but more than once he glanced about the wood,
    this way, that way, looking for Mensola.
    Oh, every murmur, every leaf astir
    caused him to think that Mensola was there.

345. 'Twas nine o' clock already of the morn,
    and Mensola was nowhere to be seen.
    But he kept waiting, waiting till the sun
    became so scorching, so unbearable
    that he no longer played with wreath or bloom,
    such was the heat that now tormented him.
    Thus, suffering and baffled all at once,
    this way, that way he raised his searching glance.

346. "Oh, can this mean that she's not coming? God!"
    he now began to moan and to lament.
    Countless odd thoughts were flashing in his mind,
    which he invented to explain his grief.
    Surely, a thousand reasons could have kept
    Mensola home! Such thing we often see
    in those who wish that something should have been,
    but think of many hurdles in between.

347. Both noon and afternoon had fled, and now
evening was vanquishing the fleeting day:
and still his Mensola had not appeared.
Bewilderment had seized Africo's heart;
therefore in great unrest, distraught and pale,
he thought that it was time for him to go.
Then to himself he whispered in dismay,
"Perhaps she met her friends along the way.

348. "She must have been detained by them all day:
my waiting longer is therefore in vain.
Night, I can see, is almost on the earth,
and a long journey lies ahead of me.
But though I've been deceived in coming here
and waiting for her in this baffling wood,
I will be back tomorrow once again."
So, to go home, he left the mountain then.

349. Three hours past noon, with a most grievous heart,
and deeply worried, Mensola awoke.
So many thoughts had tossed within her mind,
there was still terror in her open eyes.
But grief proved not so powerful a storm
as to succeed in making her forget
the promise she had made the day before—
to go to her dear Africo once more.

350. So very deeply she regretted then
all she had promised that she changed her mind.
She soon decided not to keep her word,
and nevermore to see her Africo.
Her duty was to do her very best
to hide her sin from every person's eye,
so that Diana should not know at all
when next upon her nymphs she came to call.

351. No, she could not forget her Africo,
    deep in her heart. She saw him everywhere,
    and loved him, loved him more than her own life,
    and longed with hidden fire for his kiss.
    It was Diana's fear still in her mind
    that checked her love and hampered her desire,
    preventing her from going any place
    where Africo might wait to see her face.

352. And so the second and the third day passed,
    the fourth, the fifth, the sixth, and a whole month,
    and yet not once could Africo behold
    the lovely face of her he loved so well.
    With all his anguish countless times he went
    where he had first embraced his Mensola,
    resuming on the hill his hopeless quest,
    his mind with fear and futile dreams oppressed.

353. But all his efforts were of no avail,
    till, envious of all his past delight,
    Fortune, his bitter and relentless foe,
    decided it was time to put an end
    to such a wretched and unhappy life.
    (Fortune it is that never rests an hour,
    but, turning, turning, makes man's actions go,
    and of her doings nothing seems to know.)

354. A month and more had gone, and Africo
    had never seen his Mensola again.
    His misery and grief had rendered him
    so weak and wan, so frantic and so frail
    that, ah, in all his aspect and his speech,
    he now resembled a downtrodden beast.
    His hair, once lively-gold, had now become
    all gray. About he wandered, dazed and dumb.

355. One day, as he kept watch over his flock
below the mountain, his accustomed chore,
once more his heart commanded him to go
right to the place where Mensola had vowed
she would return to him. Alone he walked,
all, all alone he wanted to go there.
Therefore, he left his copious herd behind,
and, dart in hand, went Mensola to find.

356. When to the valley and the stream he came
where he had seized and forced his Mensola,
our young man turned his glances everywhere,
"My Mensola," repeating to himself,
"I never would have thought you could betray
your faith so much. You promised me to come.
With these my very ears I heard you swear:
but not for God or me you seem to care.

357. "Don't you remember? At this very place,
your hands in mine, my hands in yours, we stood.
And it was here you falsely swore to me
you would come back; and then for a long time
I kissed your eyes, oh, now so far away,
before we bade our last farewell and left.
All your repeated promises, and all
that you kept swearing by, don't you recall?"

358. Never could I describe the many tears
Africo wept while sobbing near the stream.
To multiply his torments all the more,
he wanted to remember, one by one,
all the details of his whole loving life,
happy and sad; and it was this that made
his ancient misery far worse than ever,
till he resolved his wretchedness to sever.

359. Down to the river's edge he slowly walked,
his sharpened arrow ever in his hand.
There, on the ground he fixed the heavy shaft,
aiming its pointed steel against his breast.
"O cruel Love," he said, "because of you
I've come to this so strange, untimely death.
Rather than live a life I cannot share,
I choose to end my grief and my despair.

360. "O Father! Mother dear! Now be with God!
Into my hell of anguish I must go.
And you, O river, keep my name alive,
and let all people and all ages know
the sorrowful event about to be.
Announce to those who soon will see you flow,
limpid no more but stained with all my blood,
that I have died for Love—this cruel god."

361. This said, he called to Mensola once more,
and let himself fall heavy on his spear.
The sharp steel, piercing through the young man's heart,
instantly killed him with propitious haste.
Lifeless, his body fell into the stream,
his soul now free from suffering at last.
And soon the water through the valley flowed,
reddened by Africo's unhappy blood.

362. Not far below, the current, in those days,
as now, meandered in two separate streams.
The narrower of them, now stained with blood,
flowed right beneath the hapless lover's home.
Girafon, being at that hour outside,
noticed the crimson color of the brook,
and felt, that moment, like a sudden blow,
a strange presentiment of grief and woe.

363. Quickly and uttering no sound, he went
in the direction of his grazing flock.
Africo was not there; so slowly, slowly,
along the river bank the poor man walked
to find the place where all that blood began,
and learn at last the reason and the cause.
Whose blood was it that reddened rill and ground?
And so he came where Africo was found.

364. Ah, when he saw his son dead on the bank,
the spear still planted in his youthful breast,
he mustered all his courage not to fall,
such was the grief that overwhelmed his heart.
In great dismay he raised the lifeless arm,
saying, "Alas! Alas! O woe to me!
What cursèd hand has all this damage done?
Oh, who has dared to take your life, my son?"

365. The aged father drew him from the stream
and, sadly weeping, laid him on the bank.
He cursed that day, the worst of all his days,
crying, "My son, who looked so much like me,
what will your poor and wretched mother do
now that she's lost the only son she had?
Oh, what will be of us, my son, my lad,
so lonely now without you, and so sad?"

366. He drew the pointed spear out of his heart,
and gazed at it with sadness and in tears.
Then, in the midst of all his endless grief,
"My son," he said, "who drove this wicked steel
into your breast with all such cruelty?
Who robbed me of my bliss and of my joy?
Surely, it was Diana's enmity,
who craves the blood of my whole family."

367. Several times he gazed upon that spear,
till he admitted that it was his son's,
the one he used to carry in his hunt.
At this, with greater wretchedness, he said,
"O son! My son! My poor, unlucky son!
What suffering, what pain could be so fierce
that it should bring you to such fate and sorrow?
Who was it took your life with your own arrow?"

368. Then, after an infinity of tears,
Girafon put his child upon his back,
and carried him (he took that dart along)
with so much anguish to his lonely home.
There, to the mother, he began to tell,
weeping, still weeping, everything he knew.
That spear he showed, and said to her at last
how he had drawn it from his wounded breast.

369. Let no one, no one ask me, at this point,
how bitterly the mother whined and wept.
I could not number all her screams and tears,
I could not well describe her agony.
O lonesome mother, what distress! what pain!
She cursed her fate and all the gods above,
and, pressing now her face against her son's,
kept crying, sighing, sobbing all at once.

370. Yet in the end—for such was in those days
the funeral tradition of the land—
after more keening and more helpless tears,
and after many more heartrending cries,
they burned the body in the midst of all
the desolation of their great despair.
Their only son, their only prize and joy
inclement fate had chosen to destroy.

371. They gathered, then, the ashes of his bones—
the ashes of their child—and, finally,
walked to the stream, and saw its water red,
still red from all his blood, his hapless blood.
They dug a ditch upon the bank, and there
they buried what was left of their sweet son
so that his name might last and live forever
as long as it was carried by that river.

372. That stream was called the Africo that day,
and by this name we know it even now.
The poor old parents, now alone and sad,
lived there in utmost grief and misery.
Such was the end of gentle Africo,
and such the fame the stream inherited.
But let us leave them there, and turn to find
our Mensola, so lonesome left behind.

373. In mournful melancholy all this time
our Mensola had passed her grievous days.
But when she understood that nothing now
could alter or annul what she had done,
she grew resigned and patient in her woe.
Often she left her cavern, once again
to join the band of friends upon the hill;
often she even laughed against her will.

374. Yes, more than once she found herself with those
same nymphs who had been with her on that day
when Africo had seized her. They all knew,
oh, not about her sin, but that, that day,
they, too,—alas! alas!—had run the risk
of being taken by the daring youth.
Mensola with a tale out of her head
made them believe she, too, like them, had fled.

375. So with the passing of each coming day
Mensola grew more strongly self-assured,
seeing herself still honored and well liked
by all her friends, who thought her still to be
chaste and unsoiled as each of them was still.
Thus everyone believed the lies she told,
and her successes made her even feel
she from Diana could her sin conceal.

376. But Love could not allow her to remove
Africo from her heart to the extent
that she would not remember his sweet name
and the delight she'd tasted in his arms.
She wished that he were there, and often, too,
when least expected, she would sadly sigh.
She was in love, but thought her love a sin,
and therefore kept her flame concealed within.

377. As it had been her habit, once again
she took the spear and with her friends went hunting.
But every time she came upon the place
where Africo had held her on his breast,
with never-failing fondness she would sigh,
murmuring very softly to herself,
"You were so happy, Africo, that day
when I was yours and in your arms I lay!

378. "Now I don't know what has become of you,
but I believe you suffer for my love.
Oh, but it's not my fault, I tell you, love:
it's fear that kills all courage in my life."
As she said this, with all her heart she knew
she would have pleased her Africo once more
if someone had convinced and told her, though,
that neither nymph nor goddess was to know.

379. So, living every moment of her life
in such sweet love and yet such bitter fear,
Mensola saw her lovely face grow pale,
oh, every day more pale, as the result
of that seed flowering within her womb.
Three months went by, and she did not suspect
that she was soon to bear a little son—
which happened when her painful time was done.

380. And nature took its course. When, at the end
of the third month, her womb began to show
the fruit of her conception to her eyes,
Mensola noticed a mysterious change,
and wonderment and worry held her mind.
She failed to understand the thing she saw:
she saw her hips and her whole body grow,
but felt herself so sluggish and so slow.

381. Not knowing what was causing all of this,
Mensola was amazed, and worried more—
a simple girl who had not given birth
to any child before. And so she thought,
"What sudden illness can this ever be
that, as I notice, worsens with each hour?
Why do I every passing day grow bigger,
but lose all of my power and my vigor?"

382. On the same hillock, in a cavern deep,
no more than a half mile away from Mensola,
lived, at that time, a famous, aged nymph,
the wisest of the younger nymphs around.
She knew the healing secrets of the herbs,
and spoke on every doctrine of the world.
A hundred years of age made great her fame:
Nymph Sinedecchia was the woman's name.

383. Mensola, sweetly, to her cavern went,
and said to her, "O mother of us all,
I came for your advice." She mentioned then
the illness that was menacing her health.
Old Sinedecchia quickly shook her head,
and with the sternest face replied to her:
"Daughter, my daughter, with a man you've been,
and now you can no more conceal your sin."

384. Mensola's lovely face turned crimson-hued
when, at those words, she heard her shame exposed.
Unable to deny the open truth,
she bent her glance in timidness, and tried
to look like one half-dreaming and half-dazed.
But then she saw it was to no avail
lying to one who knew what caused her fears:
so there she stood in silence and in tears.

385. Seeing her shame and utmost misery,
but seeing, also, her great innocence,
Old Sinedecchia understood at once
that what had been, had been against her will,
and that the lass had suffered violence.
So she took pity on her fearful plight,
and, wishing then to comfort her dismay,
began to speak to her in such a way:

386. "Daughter, my daughter, such a sin as yours
cannot be hidden long, believe me. But
although you have most truly done great wrong,
I do not want you to lament so much
as to despair and die. What would you now
accomplish if you tried to take your life?
Let's see what we can do. But tell me how,
and who it was that made you break your vow."

387. Mensola uttered no reply. Instead
     as she remembered all that had occurred,
     flushed once again with shame, she hid her face,
     her lovely face, in Sinedecchia's lap.
     Her eyes resembled now two gutter-spouts
     dripping and dripping past the fallen rain.
     Oh, she could only cry, forever cry,
     unable to explain or to reply.

388. But Sinedecchia with her tender words
     insisted so that she confessed all things
     in a voice broken by new sobs and tears.
     She told her how a youth, one day, appeared,
     and tricked her with such loveliness and charm
     that she surrendered to him in the end.
     At this, she burst out crying more and more,
     invoking death as she had done before.

389. On hearing such a tale, the aged nymph
     took greater pity on the simple girl.
     She firmly knew that cunning had been used
     by that young man to trap so sweet a soul.
     First, she reproached her sternly of her sin,
     so that she would avoid all future snares:
     in order not to be deceived again,
     she was, indeed, to trust no living man.

390. Then, she succeeded with her soothing talk
     in making her no longer weep and moan.
     She even promised all her help and love
     as though she were a daughter of her own.
     At last, to tell her all that she should do,
     old Sinedecchia in this fashion spoke,
     "Now try to listen carefully, my dear,
     and pay attention to the things you hear.

391. "When nine full months have gone from the sad day
on which, alas, you were compelled to sin,
you will give birth then to a little child.
When that time comes, invoke Lucina's aid,
and the sweet goddess will soon heed your plea.
Finally, when your little babe is born,
we'll think of what's appropriate to do,
and thus take care of what is best for you.

392. "But let none of these things now vex your mind:
leave everything to me, for in my heart
I have already thought of what we need:
so let's, first, wait for your small babe to come.
Only remember: never leave this path
during these months, or else your sin will soon
be known to those who do not know it yet,
and you will suffer greater shame and threat.

393. "Hide in your cavern and remain unseen,
and wear a dress as wide as you can find,
and with no girdle, so that none may see
your body which your sin has so enlarged.
Now go in peace, and think of nothing more:
only take care, my dear, of your sweet life.
Visit me often, though, and, do not doubt it,
I'll tell you all that you should know about it."

394. Oh, the sweet solace to the maiden's ears!
She said, "O kindly mother of us all,
since I have come to this so bitter end
only because of this my shameful sin,
and since I know—how gratefully I know!—
that your advice is my one anchor left,
oh, help me, for your help I need now most,
as every other counsel I have lost."

395. "Go now," old Sinedecchia answered her,
"for I will keep my promise, to be sure.
Once more I tell you: do not worry, but
also remember: keep your sin concealed."
"I won't forget," said Mensola, her cheeks
still wet with all her tears. So she returned,
taking a shortcut, to her sunken place
with some new hope now written on her face.

396. She stayed there, all alone, in pensiveness,
and never left, as she was used to do.
Her friend, the constant friend of all her thoughts,
was Africo, and, oh, his handsome face.
Her body grew much larger every day,
but she remembered what she had to do.
Without a girdle now her dress she wore,
and went to Sinedecchia more and more.

397. Because of what was growing in her womb,
Mensola now was feeling in her heart
such love, such burning love for Africo,
that, oh, she would most willingly have run
outside to spend each passing hour with him
as when she was first caught in his desire.
Oh, why was she to hide so far away?
Crying, she called him countless times, each day.

398. It was this thought that bade her often go
back to the place of both her love and sin.
She wished to see if Africo was there,
waiting to take her home, as he had vowed.
She even found the cottage where he lived,
but fear prevented her from going near,
all, all alone: she came within its view
several times, but always then withdrew.

399. Ever in vain she looked for him, not knowing
that he had died, despairing of her love.
Meanwhile, her body had become so round
for the sweet baby living in her womb,
she could no longer move about at all.
Abandoning, therefore, her futile search,
there in her cave the coming days she passed,
because her time was now approaching fast.

400. Fortune so favored her in all this time
that none of all the nymphs that dwelt around—
and several had met her in those months—
ever found out or thought that she had sinned.
Yet some of them began, in those last days,
to wonder and to worry when they saw
their Mensola so weak, and pale, and gaunt,
and so determined not to join their hunt.

401. Diana came to Fiesole at this time,
as she had done quite often in the past.
Great was the jubilation on those hills
for the great Goddess had returned at last.
At her arrival all her nymphs rejoiced,
and gathered all together very fast,
as they were wont to do, around their queen,
eager from every region to convene.

402. Mensola knew the Goddess had arrived,
but did not dare appear before her face
in deadly fear of being ill received.
"If I go there," she thought, "how can I keep
all that has happened hidden from her eyes?
What havoc she would make of this my life!"
Also, by Sinedecchia she was bidden
stay in her cavern, more than ever hidden.

403. And so, one day, while hiding in her place,
all of a sudden Mensola began
to feel through all her body piercing pains.
The Goddess, then, of childbirth she invoked,
and a small infant boy was quickly born.
Lucina raised the baby from the ground,
tenderly placed him in her arms, and said,
"He will be great, some day," and so she fled.

404. Mensola's pains had been too fierce and vast,
too fierce and vast for a sweet, simple girl
who'd never been through such a deed before.
But when she saw that she had given birth
to such a lovely babe, her pains were gone.
As best she could, she made a tiny dress
for him at once, then suckled him at breast,
and kissed him, kissed him, unaware of rest.

405. Her baby was so darling and so dear,
so fair his face, he seemed a wonder new.
Curly and golden was his silken hair:
he was the perfect image of his sire.
Oh, look at him but once, and there you see
Africo in his eyes and in his brows.
So like his dad was he in every feature,
Mensola loved the more her newborn creature.

406. So much already did she love her child
she could not keep her gaze away from him.
Oh, not to lose a moment of her bliss,
she was unwilling to present her babe
even to Sinedecchia. Sweet illusion!
Africo seemed to be right there with her,
and so she played with him and, smiling glad,
with tender hand caressed his tiny head.

407. Diana more than once had asked her nymphs
whatever had become of Mensola.
Those who were closest to the Goddess said
it was a long, long time since on those hills
a soul had ever seen her anywhere.
Others replied that some mysterious ill
had made her feel that she no more should gaze,
like all the others, on Diana's face.

408. Therefore, one day, eager to see the one
she was so fond of and so dearly loved,
escorted by three other nymphs, Diana
walked down the hill in search of Mensola,
who, so she thought, still in her cavern lay.
Diana was the first to step inside,
certain to find her there; but she was gone:
her name was then called out by everyone.

409. Mensola with her infant at that time
was near the river, not too far below.
There, her sweet babe was playing in the sun
when suddenly she heard, so near, so near,
those voices calling, calling out her name.
She looked above, and saw Diana there,
descending fast with the escorting three;
but she had not been sighted, luckily.

410. So terror-stricken by Diana's sight
was Mensola that she could not reply.
Shaking with fear in all her body, lost,
she hid her handsome baby in a bush,
and, leaving him behind, was brave enough
to run toward safety down the lonely hill.
Holding her breath and cowering, cautious, she
from oak to sheltering oak was seen to flee.

411. But no tree hid her from Diana's eyes.
The wrathful Goddess saw her as she fled,
and, at that moment, heard the infant cry
so loudly that his crying pierced the sky.
'Twas then that with her terrifying word
Diana warned poor Mensola to stop:
"Mensola, do not run from me away!
You shall not cross the stream, if so I say.

412. "You, silly, sinful girl! You cannot shun
my arrows if I hurl them with my bow."
Mensola did not stop despite her threat,
but kept on fleeing toward the mountain's foot
until she reached the water where she plunged,
thinking that she could cross it. But Diana
whispered a magic warning to the river,
and forced him to halt Mensola forever.

413. The hapless girl, already in mid-current,
suddenly felt her feet grow weak and numb.
So then and there (Diana's wish was law)
poor Mensola dissolved into the stream
in whose cool waves she was to live forever.
In fact, that stream began to bear her name,
and as the Mensola is known today.
And now you know the tale in every way.

414. When the nymphs walking with Diana saw
poor Mensola converted into water
already with the river flowing down,
because they much had loved her in her life
they burst out crying, and began to moan,
"Oh, poor and hapless girl! Oh, wretched friend!
What grievous guilt, what horrid sin has brought her
to such a fate—a million drops of water?"

415. Diana ordered them to weep no more
for Mensola had well deserved her death.
To show them, then, the greatness of her sin,
she led them where the wailing infant lay.
She told them to remove him right away
out of the brambles where he had been left.
Out of the thickness of the bush the three
took in their arms the infant instantly.

416. They found him so delightful and so dear,
the nymphs rejoiced in gazing at his face.
They hushed his cries, and wished, deep in their hearts,
that they could take him to their mountain caves,
but none dared tell Diana of such wish.
Wasting no time, the angry Goddess bade
the child be brought to Sinedecchia's care,
and she herself with her three nymphs went there.

417. Diana let old Sinedecchia know
how she had found that infant in a bush
where Mensola, to keep her sin concealed,
had left him. "But," she added, "after this,
the little wretch a fleeting moment lived.
She was still fleeing from me, daring even
to cross the current; but the river caught her,
and, as I wished, I turned her into water."

418. While in this wise Diana spoke to her,
the aged nymph with great compassion wept,
lamenting Mensola's unhappy fate.
She took that tiny infant in her arms,
and to Diana said: "O faultless light
of all of us, I was the only one
who knew about her sin, and I alone
the truth and all her confidence had known."

419. And so she told Diana all she knew—
how Mensola had suffered violence,
and where, and how, in what ensnaring ways
she had been last deceived by some young man.
"Oh, Goddess, I assure you," she said then,
"upon my well known loyalty I swear
she would have killed herself with her own dart:
I did not let her, for she broke my heart.

420. "But since you have now turned her into water,
oh, place this tiny child within my care!
For I will take him far away from here,
down to a certain valley that I know,
where, as I well remember, once I saw
men living with their women in their homes.
I'll give this babe to them: they'll hold him dear,
and do for him what we cannot do here."

421. Hearing these truthful words, Diana learned
that Mensola had been deceived and forced,
and felt great pity in her heart at once,
for dearly she had loved her youthful nymph.
But, lest the others should forget such fate,
she still was stern, and seemed her ruthless self.
She said to Sinedecchia that she should
do for the infant everything she could.

422. With her companions she departed then,
leaving the child in Sinedecchia's care.
As soon as the great Goddess disappeared,
the aged woman, with that lovely child
tenderly on her breast, sought out the place
where he had been conceived by Mensola.
Those hills had long been home to her, and well
valley from valley, therefore, she could tell.

423. By Mensola herself she had been told
the name of the young man who had defiled her;
and she remembered she had also heard
in what direction he had gone away.
Therefore, now bearing all these things in mind,
she came to the conclusion that the lad
came from the dell where she had once caught sight
of a cottage with smoke rising from its height.

424. Down to that valley painfully she walked,
and Alimena luckily was there.
"O dearest friend," the aged nymph began,
"sorrowful business brings me to your home,
yet I am forced to tell you what it is.
Therefore, I beg you, do not be dismayed
by the sad story that you will now hear
about the birth of this sweet infant dear."

425. Then she repeated everything she knew—
how a young man, named Africo, one day,
forced a young nymph. She even told her where,
and how the whole thing happened, and how long
the wretched lass had roamed from hill to hill
until that lovely, luscious fruit was ripe;
and how, and where angry Diana caught her,
turning the luckless maiden into water;

426. and how Diana herself had, later, found
that infant crying underneath a bush,
and how he was entrusted to her care.
As she was telling these and other things,
the baby's face caught Alimena's eyes.
She said, "This child looks so much like my son,
so much like my poor Africo. Oh, look!"
and in her arms the little child she took.

427. Oh, she began to weep great tears of joy
 as she kept gazing on the infant's face:
 her Africo was there, alive again,
 her dear, dear son had finally returned.
 She kissed him, with great love she kissed him more,
 saying, "It's hard for me, it breaks my heart
 to tell you, O my little pretty one,
 about your father's death, my only son."

428. Then she began to tell the aged nymph
 all that there was to tell about her son—
 in what great anguish a long time he lived,
 and what a sad and bitter death he died.
 Old Sinedecchia, at that story, wept,
 moaning the fate of gentle Africo,
 and in her tears his saddened mother shared
 when Girafone at that point appeared.

429. He, also, when the story was retold,
 openly wept from happiness and grief.
 He, too, looked at the infant: oh, indeed,
 he was the perfect image of his son.
 Never was he so happy in his life.
 As he began to fondle and to feast
 his grandson with great tenderness, the child,
 moved by his instinct, looked at him and smiled.

430. So great was their rejoicing and their bliss,
 so sudden and so simple their delight
 that, were it not for the still grieving thought
 of the two lovers, still so young to die,
 their gladness would, indeed, have been complete.
 Old Sinedecchia soon made friends with them;
 but it was time for her to say farewell,
 and find again her mountain, there to dwell.

431. Girafon thanked her a full thousand times,
and Alimena warmly thanked her, too,
for the good service she had rendered them,
and they both honored her, and thanked her more.
As warmly Sinedecchia answered them
over and over; wasting, then, no time,
she left their home, and went back to her cave,
but that sweet child to his grandparents gave.

432. The news spread fast around from hill to hill,
and so in all that region it was known
that Mensola had been turned into water,
which made so many nymphs weep tears of grief.
Some time elapsed, and great Diana chose
to leave that place and seek another land.
She left that countryside but not before
bidding her band be chaste forevermore.

433. She gave the same old warning to her nymphs,
who called that stream the Mensola thereafter.
But back to Girafone and Alimena!
They reared the little infant on the milk
from their own flock, and with great sacrifice,
and called the child Prunèo (from the bush
where he had been found crying), and that name
was to remain throughout his future fame.

434. Pruneo grew so winsome and so fair,
nature herself, had she employed the best
of all her power to paint her fairest form,
could not have made a more delightful youth.
He was more nimble than a lion cub,
incomparably strong and brave was he:
in brief, he so resembled his dead father
that people thought him the same person, rather.

435. Both Girafon and Alimena watched
over him day and night with boundless care,
and more than often they revealed to him
how Africo, his sire, had met his death.
They wanted, thus, their grandson to abhor
the selfsame woodland that had caused such grief
to both his parents: everything they told
Pruneo, who was now eighteen years old.

436. It was the time when Attalante came
with a great army to this part of Europe,
and ultimately seized all Tuscany.
As all our chronicles most clearly show,
'twas Appollinus who, with great insight,
saw that the neighboring plain of Fiesole
was, for its valley and as well its height,
the most propitious European site.

437. So Attalante ordered in that place
a city built, which Fiesole was named.
And it was then his men began to seize
some of the nymphs they found upon those hills,
for those who did not fall into their hands
vanished and fled from their old countryside.
And so some nymphs were chased out of their dens,
and others grabbed and married off at once.

438. Then Attalante ruled that the inhabitants
of all that land should in the city live.
When Girafone heard the happy news,
he, too, like all the others, left his home,
taking his brave and handsome lad along—
his dear Pruneo, virtuous and kind—
and Alimena. To Attalante he went,
and bowed to him, loyal and reverent.

439. When Attalante saw the aged man,
     he welcomed him with warmth and courtesy.
     He took his hand as though they were old friends,
     and then addressed him with these gracious words,
     "O wise old man, hear what I have to say!
     I on my word of honor swear to you
     that, if you choose this town and live with me,
     one of my greatest counselors you'll be.

440. "In this my fortress you will live with me,
     together with this handsome son of yours."
     Girafon answered promptly with these words,
     "O Attalante, if you so command,
     my counsel will be quick to heed your voice.
     But with such prudent men around your throne
     I wonder whether I may ever be
     able to give you what you ask of me."

441. "Yes, I have prudent men around my throne,"
     good Attalante smilingly replied;
     "but since, as I know well, you've lived so long
     around these valleys and around these hills,
     and, therefore know the things that one should know,
     both good and bad, of all this region, then
     I'm sure the best advice can come from you
     about a country that to me is new."

442. Girafon, almost on the verge of tears,
     said, "Attalante, oh, you are so right.
     I am an old, old man, and my sad life,
     indeed, can prove that all I say is true.
     'Twas in this region, not too long ago,
     that with my wife I spent my days in grief,
     when people brought to me this darling one,
     who is the son of my unhappy son."

443. He told him, then, the story as it was,
about his Africo and his dear Mensola;
also, about Mugnone, caught and killed
by stern Diana. All his ancient woes
he thus narrated, pointing out to him
the rivers that he mentioned, north and south,
and more than once explaining how it came
to pass that each of them had such a name.

444. Turning to Attalante, then he said:
"My lord, I am most eager to obey."
Good Attalante thanked him for all this;
then, gazing on Pruneo fixedly,
and, liking him too dearly, bade him come,
and tenderly addressed the handsome youth,
"My lad, for my love's sake, I hope you're able
to be my gracious servant at my table."

445. Thus Girafon was made a counselor
by Attalante, while our young Pruneo,
chosen to do so, waited on his lord.
So well did he perform his given task,
all people looked at him, amazed and pleased.
Nature, beyond all this, had made our youth
so bold and strong that it was hard to find
his peer in games or jousts of any kind.

446. Expert in hunting and by far the best,
so agile and so swift in every move,
so quick in leaping, that no savage beast
could ever come before him and still live.
With such precision he could aim his bow
he could have won Diana at her sport.
But he was also so well mannered, so
pleasing that my best word can hardly show.

447. Soon Attalante grew so fond of him,
seeing the lad so valiant and so wise,
he named him Seneschal, and placed him high
above his people and above his land.
Thus he became the country's governor,
and with such charm and gentleness he ruled,
everyone loved him; for all people knew
his never-failing law: to each his due.

448. When he was more than twenty-five years old,
good Attalante chose for him a bride,
a lovely girl whose name was Tironèa,
the daughter of a mighty, noble baron
sojourning in his court. His wedding gift
was all the region that between the banks
of the Mugnon and the Mensola lay—
a lovely present for a lovely day.

449. Then, at Maiano, almost next its church,
Pruneo had a mighty castle built.
He viewed the entire plainland from that height,
which he made strong with battlements around.
And in no time at all, as I've been told,
he tamed a country that was once most wild.
This he accomplished, as I understand,
for the great love he bore his native land.

450. Much of his time upon that hill he passed,
dwelling forever in delight and bliss.
Often, the legend says, he went to see
the rivers that recalled his parents' names,
and with their spirits there he paused to talk,
while from the streams came voices clear and true,
and heavy sighs, and moans, and murmurings,
telling a mournful tale of ancient things.

451. Repaid for all his sorrows, Girafon
lived a long time. But when his life arrived,
ah, to the last of all its long, long years,
he from this world departed, leaving here
his Alimena weeping with much woe.
When she died too, she soon was laid to rest
in the same sepulcher with Girafon
there in the town that had become their own.

452. Pruneo ruled and lived in high esteem
together with his lovely Tironèa.
They had ten children, each of them so brave
and so well mannered—a delight to see.
And all of them were married in due time,
and so their progeny far larger grew.
All citizens of Fiesole, far greater
they were than all their neighbors, then and later.

453. When our Pruneo died, amid the tears
of the whole populace, he was interred.
Therefore that region, liberal and free—
good Attalante's gift to him alone—
was ruled and governed by his many sons.
They shared it equally among themselves,
and from that day they were in full command
of Fiesole and all its neighboring land.

454. But Fiesole surrendered to the Romans,
and was, for the first time, razed to the ground.
Many defected to the Roman side,
but Africo's descendants did not yield.
They gathered all around the fortress built
by their Pruneo a long time ago,
and there they settled, just as in the past
building new homes and shelters, bold and fast.

455. The Romans founded Florence not too far,
so that old Fiesole would not survive,
despite its noble, strong inhabitants,
determined not to live anywhere else.
And that was why the Fiesolani went
from place to savage place—an exiled throng,
a nomad populace, eager to find
a home, a hut, and help of any kind.

456. But when, past many years, the old wrath died
in every heart and mind, and peace was made
between the Romans and the banished throng,
nearly all men resolved to go to dwell
in Florence, in the might of her great walls.
Thus Africo's descendants went there, too,
greeted and warmly welcomed with great cheer
by the whole town, and held forever dear.

457. And, so that they no longer might expect
any more damage, any further harm,
and so that they might find a greater cause
for loving, and be loved by, their new land,
not only were their grievances erased,
but intermarriages were started soon:
they loved each other, shared all wealth and worth,
and thus to a great city they gave birth.

458. So Florence grew in populace and wealth,
and, thanks to her new power and new worth,
ruled in serenity a long, long time.
But, as we all have learned from many a book,
the Christian creed had come into her walls
when Totila arrived and seized the town,
dismantled, razed each stronghold to the ground,
and banished those who still alive were found.

459. 'Twas then Fiesole's walls and citadels
were built by cruel Totila once more.
Throughout the land he had his order read
that all those persons who returned at once
to live within the walls of Fiesole
would be protected from all future harm
provided that, to please their lord, they swore
on Rome and all her lands eternal war.

460. But Africo's descendants showed their scorn
and indignation, and did not return.
Instead, they all remained right in the land
lying below their first and ancient hill.
There each of them had built his dwelling-place,
and there they raised a bastion of great might
because of which they would protected be
from Fiesole and all its enmity.

461. And in that place they stayed a long, long time
till the good monarch Charlemagne arrived
to succor all of Italy, and aid
the city of Rome, that in the meantime had
gone through much suffering. Africo's men
gathered together, came to council with
the other nobles who away had run,
and on these things were all agreed upon:

462. To send an envoy quickly to the Pope
in Rome and to their sovereign Charlemagne,
to let them know how things were faring there—
that their great daughter languished on the ground
in havoc and despair, and that in tears
her citizens were forced to leave their walls,
and that, of Fiesole once more afraid,
they could not have their walls or homes remade.

463. But I must here be brief because this tale
is clearly written in another book.
Because of that envoy, the Holy Father
remembered Florence, and his heart was moved.
And when victorious Charlemagne returned,
he visited our regions one by one,
built Florence once again with no delay,
which kept expanding to this very day.

464. Because of all these facts, Africo's race
returned with all the others to live there.
How then they grew and prospered ever since,
from branch to branch, I cannot now describe.
But this I know: that men of great renown,
from lineage to lineage, came down,
while others, too, descend from that same tree
although they seem a different family.

465. But be that as it may, I now have come
into my longed-for harbor finally,
where my desire and all my thoughts of love,
weary of boundless oceans, wished to be.
Here I lay down my weary pen to rest,
for I have done what I was asked to do
by one who rules my soul with such command
that not at all could I his wish withstand.

466. Therefore, at the conclusion of my work,
I wish to dedicate it to the one
who gave me all my strength, and all his help,
and all my style and power to write and rhyme—
to Love, I say, whose faithful slave I am,
and shall forever be. I'll go to him,
to bring this book, and thank him where he is,
and also proffer my apologies:

467. "O highest of all lords, O sovereign Love,
whose might and majesty and magnitude
control and govern every human heart,
and who are such that no one on this earth,
however base, barbaric, or uncouth,
defies without being suddenly subdued
if so you wish (though more is your delight
when gentle hearts alone yield to your might):

468. "you are the one who, should you so decide,
can bring all sadness to a sudden bliss;
you are the only one who can dispense,
if so you choose, both enmity and peace;
you, you alone destroy your servants' hearts
and often raise them suddenly from death;
you, only you condemn or yet condone,
you, only you make people smile or moan.

469. "One of your servants—and a loyal one,
I have been ordered solemnly by you
to tell this story. Eager to obey,
for I am one a lady holds in thrall,
I've finally concluded with your help
the book you bade me write. Oh, here it is,
made possible by what my mind has learned
and what for all my service I have earned.

470. "But now most fervently I beg you, Love:
grant and command, and let it be your wish,
that this my book be read by none on earth
whose life is ruled by ignorance and hate.
Those who have never known that you exist,
and, worse than this, seem not to care at all,
will surely scorn the lovely tale I write,
and hold your inspiration in great spite.

471. "Let this my book be read by gentle souls,
by those who bear your emblem on their brows,
by sweet and humble and angelic hearts
where you still reign in all your majesty.
These, these alone will not despise your deeds,
but will, instead, accept them with their praise.
So take my book. I offer now to you
what to your lordship is forever due."

472. "Let my most faithful servant come to me
before the others who obey my law.
Without the burning longings of his heart
never could he have finished this my book.
I am so sure it's such as I desired,
I willingly accept it. In a safe
I'll lock it, where I keep the documents
of my best deeds and mightiest events.

473. "With all my heart I grant you what you ask,
for I am deeply moved by such a plea.
I shall forever guard this book you wrote
from those who never served me, as you say,
oh, not because I fear their blab at all
or in the least resent their faithless hearts,
but just to keep my name unsoiled by these
unworthy people. And go now in peace!"

THE LIBRARY
ST. MARY'S COLLEGE OF MARYLAND
ST. MARY'S CITY, MARYLAND 20686

087647

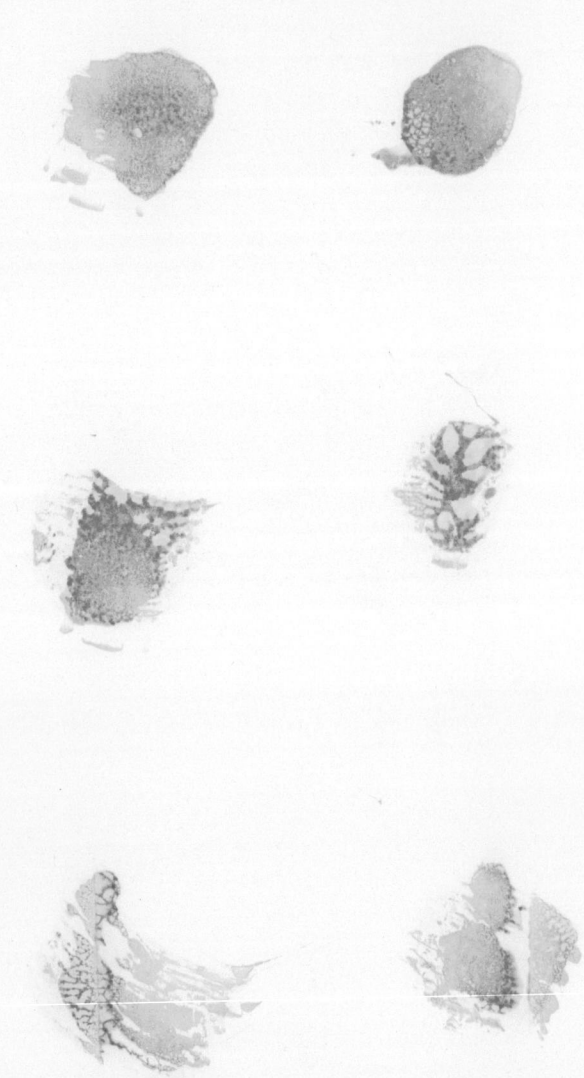